Kenyan Student Airlifts to America

1959-1961

An Educational Odyssey

T0319197

Robert F Stephens

Kenway Publications

Published by
Kenway publications
an imprint of
East African Educational Publishers Ltd.
Brick Court, Mpaka Road/Woodvale Grove
Westlands, P.O. Box 45314
Nairobi – 00100
KENYA

email: eaep@eastafricanpublishers.com
website: www.eastafricanpublishers.com

East African Educational Publishers Ltd.
C/O Gustro Ltd.
P.O. Box 9997, Kampala
UGANDA

Ujuzi Books Ltd.
P.O. Box 38260, Dar es Salaam
TANZANIA

East African Publishers Rwanda Ltd.
Tabs Plaza, Kimironko Road,
Opposite Kigali Institute of Education
P.O. Box 5151, Kigali
RWANDA

ISBN 978-9966-25-930-1

Printed in Kenya by
Printwell Industries Ltd.
P.O. Box 5216-0506
Nairobi, Kenya

Contents

Epigraph

"The new African nations are determined to educate their people – maintain their independence and receive the respect of all the world ... To meet the need for education, we must greatly increase the number of African students – future African leaders – brought to this country for university training."

John F Kennedy
Bowling Green,
Kentucky,
8 October 1960

Foreword

Iam greatly honoured to be asked by Robert F Stephens to write a Foreword for this book. I met him first in early 1958 soon after the examination results for the Overseas Cambridge School Certificate were announced. I had just qualified to go to Makerere University in Uganda to study medicine. But I wanted to be an engineer and to study in the United States of America. I explained my desires to Dr Gikonyo Kiano, who was at the time a lecturer at the newly founded Royal Technical College, Nairobi. He introduced me to Robert Stephens.

Dr Stephens was very inspiring and supportive. In a colonial and racially governed Kenya, it was refreshing to meet a white man, who was not a missionary, supporting young Africans to obtain university education overseas. Because of the efforts of Dr Stephens, Thomas J Mboya, and Dr Julius Gikonyo Kiano, I and young men like me, including Barrack Obama Sr, whom I knew well, found our way to America and subsequently helped establish a stronger bond between Kenya and the United States.

The airlifts opened the developed world of North America to many talented young Kenyans. A number of our top professors and lecturers in Kenyan universities were trained in America, not to mention the dozens working in government and the private sector. As Chancellor of the University of Nairobi from 2004, which by 2013 had a population of over 60,000 students and still growing, I appreciate the impact that American university education has had on our economic, social and political development. Many years after the airlifts, young Kenyans still seek opportunities to study in America. Of my six children, five had their university education in the USA.

There have been several efforts to write this story. In particular, I know that the late Dr Kiano and H E Ambassador Pamela Mboya were keen to see these events recorded. Dr Stephens is to be commended for putting on paper a true story of what has helped shape the present day Kenya.

This book is in many ways a tribute to two visionary Kenyans: Thomas J Mboya and Dr Julius Gikonyo Kiano. Both men were my friends and I believe they would be rightly proud of the results of their vision and hard work.

Joe Barrage Wanjui
CBS, Chancellor of the University
Nairobi
August 2013

Preface

Robert Stephens has written an absorbing book about pre-independence Kenya. What did it take to get hundreds of Kenyan students, thirsting for higher education, into USA colleges in the late 1950s and early 1960s? It took perseverance, help from countless people, and the overwhelming desire of the students themselves. The extraordinary efforts of one Kenyan leader, Tom Mboya, were crucial.

The airlifts were an excellent example of successful cultural diplomacy. Every person on the lifts benefited from their American education, and most became lasting friends of the USA. They learnt a work ethic, became self-reliant and self-confident, and returned to Kenya during the time of their country's independence. They served both in the new government and in the private sector. Most notable was the large number of women who were part of the initial airlift. Up to that time almost no African women went to foreign colleges, but the airlifts changed this. The women did as well in the USA as the men.

Dr Robert F Stephens and I were both Cultural Affairs Officers in Kenya. We were known as the officers who "handled scholarships". When we were out in public, we were surrounded by students who desperately wanted to go to college in the United States. Their desire for an education was palpable. It is gratifying that the airlifts proved so successful. Dr Stephens has told his riveting story with great skill to appeal both to those who were part of that experience, and to a new generation of African youth.

I personally see the book as something of a permanent tribute to Dr Julius Kiano, Kariuki Njiiri, and Tom Mboya. One of the outstanding figures of his generation, Mr Mboya is now largely forgotten. As Dr Stephens shows, it was Mr Mboya's foresight, democratic enlightenment, and diplomatic skills that played the critical role.

Dr Jack H Mower
JH Mower Associates
Consultants on Africa

Endorsements

This is an engaging and insightful book about an important and ignored slice of history. When we think of vital historical airlifts, minds race back to the Berlin Airlift. Robert Stephens takes us to another American-sponsored airlift that brought a generation of future African leaders to our shores for higher education. This effort profoundly altered the lives of these men and women, the development of East African nations, and the perception of America. At a time when the world struggled to understand the value of 'soft' as opposed to military power, this book offers a valuable historical model.

Ken Auletta
Author and Columnist for The New Yorker

I found *Kenyan Student Airlifts to America, 1959-1961: An Educational Odyssey* a fascinating narrative. It fills in more than a few things regarding both that period of Kenyan-US relations as well as Dr Stephens' very personal engagement with the whole venture. Set during the last days of colonialism in Kenya, the book documents the development of human talent that would foster a majority-ruled independent Kenya. Its focus on Africans – their individual and collective biographies, aspirations and intermittent assistance from the US and others – is the story.

Dr E Phillip Morgan Professor Emeritus
Former Dean of International Policy and Development
Monterey Institute of International Studies

Kenyan Student Airlifts to America, 1959-1961: An Educational Odyssey rings with authenticity and human concern, and is an invaluable chronicle of the airlifts and the stories of individual successes and failures.

E Jefferson Murphy
Former Five College Professor of African Studies
Former Visiting Lecturer in Social Anthropology,
University College of Fort Hare

Acknowledgements

I would like to thank Dr Julius Gikonyo Kiano, Evanson Gichuhi, Lucas Kuria, and Gloria Hagberg for their invaluable assistance in helping me track down so many of the East African Airlifters.

Thanks too to Dr Joseph and Ann Wanjui for their hospitality and assistance during stays in Nairobi while I was conducting my interviews. I also wish to thank Professor Joyce Ross and fellow writers Elisabeth Clark, Rob Dinsmoor, Linda Finigan, Beth Hogan, Elenita Lodge, and Tina Varinos for their invaluable feedback through several drafts of this book. My wife Dorothy provided endless patience and support, as well as significant editorial assistance in making this book a reality. Above all, I will be forever grateful to all those American-educated Kenyans who so generously shared their memories and their time in telling the stories of their experiences in America.

Robert Stephens
August 2013

Abbreviations

AA	–	Associate of Arts
AAI	–	African American Institute
AASF	–	African-American Students Foundation
ACOA	–	American Committee on Africa
AFL–CIO	–	American Federation of Labour and Congress
IO	–	Industrial Organisations
AID	–	Agency for International Development
AS	–	Associate of Science
ASPAU	–	African Scholarship Programme of American Universities
BAT	–	British American Tobacco Company
CECA	–	Council for Educational Cooperation with Africa
CID	–	Criminal Investigation Department
CLSMB	–	Cotton Lint and Seed Marketing Board
CPA	–	Certified Public Accountant
EACSO	–	East African Common Services Organisation
ICDC	–	Industrial and Commercial Development Corporation
IIE	–	Institute of International Education
KANU	–	Kenya African National Union
KAPE	–	Kenya African Preliminary Examination
KAU	–	Kenya African Union
KCA	–	Kikuyu Central Association
KEF	–	Kenya Education Fund
KEPC	–	Kenya Export Promotion Council
KFA	–	Kenya Farmers Association
KICC	–	Kenyatta International Convention Centre
KICD	–	Kenya Institute of Curriculum Development
KIE	–	Kenya Institute of Education
KNCCI	–	Kenya National Chamber of Commerce and Industry
KNTC	–	Kenya National Trading Corporation
NAACP	–	National Association for the Advancement of Coloured People
NCST	–	National Council for Science and Technology

OAU	–	Organisation of African Unity
OWU	–	Ohio Wesleyan University
PAFMECA	–	Pan-African Freedom Movement for East, Central, and South Africa
PhD	–	Doctor of Philosophy
SUNY	–	State University of New York
TV	–	Television
UN	–	United Nations
UNEP	–	United Nations Environment Programme
UNESCO	–	United Nations Educational, Scientific and Cultural Organisation
USA	–	United States of America
USAID	–	United States Agency for International Development
USD	–	United States Dollar(s)
USIS	–	United States Information Service

Introduction

In 1957, to quote British Prime Minister Harold MacMillan, the "... winds of change were sweeping across Africa." Ghana would become independent that same year, Nigeria in 1960. In Kenya, these same winds fanned the flame of African demands for their own independence from Britain. African-Kenyans understood that one avenue to achieving this goal and preparing themselves to govern an independent Kenya lay in education – particularly higher education, long denied by the British colonial government to the vast majority of Africans. With the end of the Mau Mau rebellion in sight, and the easing of travel restrictions, many young men and women sought opportunities for higher education beyond Kenya's borders – in South Africa, India, the United States of America (USA) and Canada.

I was posted to Nairobi in November, 1957, as Vice Consul and Cultural Affairs Officer with the United States Information Service (USIS), and was almost immediately swept up in the all-out effort of these young Kenyans to find admission and scholarship-aid in USA colleges and universities. By the end of 1958, I had been privileged to assist in the departure of nine students on official USA Government scholarships and of thirty one others who left privately.

In 1959, the numbers swelled dramatically. Each morning brought long queues of would-be students outside my office door, all hoping for any advice and help I could give. One by one I interviewed them, and then sent them to the USIS library where they pored through American college catalogues sent away for applications, and brought me the completed forms for final review. I encouraged, counselled and advised to the best of my ability.

In September 1959, thanks to the fundraising efforts of a handful of young African leaders and some American friends, one hundred twenty six students (eighty one on the first East African Student Airlift plus an additional forty five who left in other ways) departed for the USA to join the few Kenyans who were already enrolled in various North American institutions of higher learning.

The 1959 Student Airlift was the first of three, the first two supported primarily by private donations, that over the course of three years afforded a determined group of young Kenyans the opportunity for higher education in the USA.

What follows is a truly remarkable story, not only of the few who had gone earlier, but of the hundreds of Kenyans who went to colleges and universities in the USA and Canada from 1957 to 1961. What makes the story unique is that this influx of Kenyans probably represented the largest wave of international students to arrive from a single country in so short a space of time. Their impact on Kenya before and after independence in 1963 set Kenya apart from the chaos in other African countries at the time. The American-educated graduates played a vital role in the social, economic, and political modernisation of the new nation – and in the transformation of what had been for the Africans a peasant society solely dependent on subsistence agriculture into a modern democracy.

Such an unusual set of events comprised a tale that needed to be told, and led to the writing of this book. It is based on records I kept at the time, both in Nairobi and later when I returned in January, 1960 to the Cultural Affairs Division of the State Department in Washington DC as Chief of Educational and Cultural Affairs for Eastern and Southern Africa.

From 1987-88, and again in 1996, I conducted follow-up interviews in Nairobi with as many graduates of American and Canadian universities as I could track down. Because of the proximity of Central region to Nairobi the capital city, greater numbers of candidates from the Central Kenya applied for scholarships and seats on the airlifts. However, every effort was made to ensure that individuals from other regions and ethnic groups, including the Luo, Luhya, Taita, Maasai, Nandi, Giriama and Kisii were interviewed and their stories told. Hearing and recording all the stories, I was impressed by the students' determination and hard work, their many accomplishments, and their reports of the unprecedented way in which Americans (Canadians also) stepped forward to welcome, house, provide for, and educate these often penniless African students about whom they knew next to nothing but whom they were more than willing to help.

This brief history of their educational odyssey celebrates the foresight and dedication of the many young Kenyans who returned home after their studies, well prepared to build their new nation.

Robert Stephens
August 2013

Kenway autobiographies

1. *A Fly in Amber*, Susan Wood
2. *A Love Affair with the Sun*, Michael Blundell
3. *Facing Mount Kenya*, Jomo Kenyatta
4. *From Simple to Complex: The Journey of a Herdsboy*, Prof Joseph Maina Mungai
5. *Illusion of Power*, GG Kariuki
6. *The Mediator: General Sumbeiywo and the Sudan Peace Process*, Waithaka Waihenya
7. *Madatally Manji: Memoirs of a Biscuit Baron*, Madatally Manji
8. *My Journey Through African Heritage*, Allan Donvan
9. *Nothing but the Truth*, Yusuf K Dawood
10. *Tales from Africa*, Douglas Collins
11. *Theatre Near the Equator*, Annabel Maule
12. *The Southern Sudan: Struggle for Liberty*, Elijah Malok
13. *Wings of the Wind*, Valerie Cuthbert
14. *Tom Mboya: The Man Kenya Wanted to Forget*, David Goldsworthy
15. *Not Yet Uhuru*, Jaramogi Oginga Odinga
16. *Freedom and After*, Tom Mboya
17. *Dreams in a Time of War*, Ngũgĩ wa Thiong'o
18. *Beyond Expectations: From Charcoal to Gold*, Njenga Karume with Mutu wa Gethoi
19. *A Profile of Kenyan Entreprenuers*, Wanjiru Waithaka and Evans Majeni
20. *Running for Black Gold: Fifty Years of African Athletics*, Kevin Lillis
21. *Kiraitu Murungi: An Odyssey in Kenyan Politics*, Peter Kagwanja with Humphrey Ringera
22. *In the House of the Interpreter*, Ngũgĩ wa Thiong'o
23. *Kenyan Student Airlifts to America, 1959-1961: An Educational Odyssey*, Robert F Stephens

Chapter 1

Kenya in context

A brief geography and history of East Africa

East Africa, encompassing Kenya, Uganda and Tanzania, covers approximately 1,916,593 square kilometres, which makes it about the size of the United States east of the Mississippi River minus New England and Florida. Kenya, with an area of 582,748 square kilometres, is a bit smaller than Texas State in the USA. Being a country of contrasts, its dry, barren bush gives way to grassy plains abundant with wild animals, rolling green hills covered with coffee and tea plantations, and a towering snow-capped Mount Kenya.

The capital city, Nairobi, meaning 'cool waters' in Maasai, lies at an altitude of 1,680 metres. It is just 145 kilometres south of the Equator, which bisects the country. The city was established almost by accident. In 1896 the British had begun an ambitious project of building a railroad from the port of Mombasa on the Coast of the Indian Ocean to Lake Victoria and Uganda, eight hundred and five kilometres away. The goal was to provide transportation and stimulate commerce between the Coast and the interior of Africa. Four hundred and eighty three kilometres from the Coast, the Great Rift Valley lay before them – a formidable engineering obstacle. The engineers and builders established a base camp where materials could be stored and workshops built for the daunting assault on the Rift. That makeshift supply station eventually became the city of Nairobi.

Over the years, with the advent of air travel, Nairobi was well placed to become a North/South hub of traffic and commerce. Until 1959, however, the only sizeable airport was Eastleigh, a former Royal Air Force base with Quonset huts[1] for a terminal and one dirt runway that churned up huge clouds of red dust with every takeoff and landing. When the new Nairobi Embakasi Airport (now Jomo Kenyatta International Airport) was opened in May 1958, traffic from Europe and the Middle East made Nairobi a major stop en route to and from South Africa and India.

---

1 A military shelter made of corrugated steel sheet, with a semicircular cross section.

Because of its altitude, Nairobi's climate is moderate. The two rainy seasons are cool and it is only during the hottest part of the year – January and February – that the full intensity of the sun is felt. Even then, stepping into a shady spot under a tree has a soothing cooling effect. There is no need for air conditioning. To the contrary, in July and August a fire in the fireplace is most welcome.

The population of Kenya is a rich mix of forty two ethnic groups, the result of complex movements of peoples that took place over centuries, with frequent intermingling and the formation of new groups, languages and cultures. Nairobi's immediate vicinity was almost entirely populated by the largest single ethnic group, the Kikuyu. Farmers by tradition, they held much of the best arable land on the high Central plateau and so were most affected by British settlement in the highlands. Land ownership became the basis of intractable conflict between them and the British settlers. An intelligent, progressive, and dynamic people, the Kikuyu were quick to grasp the political and economic implications of the colonial incursion and the loss of their land. They responded with a rising insistence on their rights and a demand for education. Inevitably, given their proximity, the two societies rubbed each other raw.

American contacts with East Africa go back to the early 1800s with the arrival of East Indiamen merchant ships from Salem, Massachusetts, on their way to the Far East. In 1836 a United States Consulate was opened in the Sultanate of Zanzibar. An exotic island famous for its aromatic cloves, Zanzibar lay off the Coast of what later became British East Africa. Eighteen of the first twenty one consuls posted there were New Englanders and all but two were from Massachusetts, attesting to the long trade relationship between New England and East Africa.

Nevertheless, in spite of the trade between the USA and the East African Coast including Zanzibar, most people in the Americas knew little about that part of Africa. Unlike West Africa, better known as the place where the ancestors of most African Americans were taken as slaves, human trade in East Africa was mainly in the hands of Arab slavers. Most of their slaves were destined for the Middle East or India, although a few were sent to Brazil during Portuguese rule in Mozambique.

The interior of East Africa remained largely unknown until European exploration began in the 1850s, followed by the 1884-85 Berlin Congress when, Britain and Germany divided the area between themselves. Kenya went to the British while Tanganyika went to the Germans.

Meanwhile American interests in East Africa had been sparked by newspaper accounts of the drama of Henry Stanley Morton, a reporter for *The New York Herald Tribune*, and his search for the supposedly lost missionary, explorer David Livingstone. He 'found' him in 1871 on the shores of Lake Tanganyika, giving rise to the famous quote in the *Tribune*: "Dr Livingstone, I presume?"

Further attention was focused on East Africa in 1909, when America was intrigued by the adventures of Theodore Roosevelt who, after his presidency, came on a hunting safari. Several years later, in 1918, the first USA Consulate office opened in Nairobi, but during the decades that followed, through the 1930s and 1940s, America's view of that part of the world was shaped largely by movies like 'Tarzan of the Apes'[2] and 'Jungle Jim'.[3]

In the early 1950s, the bloody uprising called 'Mau Mau' caught the attention of many Americans. Most had only vague notions of what it was unless by chance they had read Robert Ruark's novel, *Something of Value*. The novel was based on events that took place in the Kenya Colony during the violent Mau Mau insurrection of the 1950s. Ruark's portrait of this African fight for independence, and the movie that followed, were complete with grisly descriptions of murder, rape and torture on both sides of the conflict during which thousands of Africans died or were put in detention. By the late 1950s, the Mau Mau rebellion was coming to an end, though some of the freedom fighters were still being hunted down in the mountains outside Nairobi. A state of emergency would remain in effect until January, 1960.

During the post World War II years, United States leaders – President Eisenhower and his Secretary of State John Foster Dulles as well as others, virtually ignored Africa. Dulles' dealings with Africa were almost exclusively through the European colonial powers, filtered through the Bureau of European Affairs. Not surprisingly, the road to Africa, including Kenya, led through London, Paris, Lisbon, and Brussels and generally stopped there. Information gained was subject to European colonial mindsets and interpretations. Not until 1958 was a Bureau of African Affairs established in the US State Department.

Back in Kenya, the settlers' hold on land in the Central highlands continued to grow despite the fact that the British Government had actually recognised, in 1923, the primacy of African interests in Kenya. In the Devonshire White Paper, His Majesty's government had stated

---

2   Tarzan of the Apes was a series of movies based on books by Edgar Rice Burroughs about a child raised in the African jungle by apes.

3   Jungle Jim was the fictional hero in a series of jungle adventures that began in 1934 as an American newspaper comic strip and later appeared in radio, film and TV.

"... that the interests of the African native must be paramount, and that if and when those interests and the interests of the immigrant races should conflict, the former should prevail." Over the years this commitment was honoured more in the breach than in the observance, but the policy remained as a stated objective and eventually became the cornerstone of the changes that would accelerate throughout the late 1950s and early 1960s.

Unfortunately, African education in Kenya had not been a matter of great concern to the British. Settlement by whites had been stimulated quite dramatically after World War I by the offer of free land in Kenya to war veterans, and since then most affairs had been left entirely in the hands of the settlers. Although in 1911 the colonial government had set up a Department of Education for children of white settlers, no schools were provided for Africans. The settlers only need was for cheap manual labour, and they opposed literacy for Africans. As one settler said, "It would only put foolish notions in their ... heads." African education was left to the missionaries. Thus, for five million Africans, only a few primary schools and four high schools had been established by various church groups.

The first secondary school, Alliance High School, was started in 1926 by an alliance of Protestant religious groups: Anglican, Church of Scotland, African Inland Mission, and United Methodists. In 1927, the second Catholic Holy Ghost Mission High School at Mang'u was founded followed in the 1930s by the Protestant Maseno Secondary School and the Catholic St Mary's High School at Yala.

Together, these four schools could take only a small number of the primary school graduates who had been able to pass the Kenya African Preliminary Examination (KAPE), the rigorous school-leavers exam. For the few who did go on, the limited secondary education received at one of the African high schools was terminal. It did not lead to the Cambridge Higher School Certificate needed for admission to a British university.

The first Kenyan African to obtain a college degree

Despite all this, one Alliance graduate unearthed a way to circumvent the roadblocks to further education. Peter Mbiyu Koinange, the son of a Kikuyu Senior Chief, was a member of the very first Alliance High School class of 1926. By any standards, his achievements were remarkable. He was the first Kenyan to study in the United States and the first East African ever to obtain a degree anywhere. With the help of the Phelps-Stokes Fund, a philanthropic foundation in New York, he was accepted in 1927 at Hampton Institute in Virginia, and with aid from his father and from Hampton, he earned an American high school diploma. In 1931, again helped by American friends, he entered Ohio Wesleyan University (OWU) and received a Bachelor of Arts degree. He then went on to Columbia University Teachers College for a master's degree in teacher education.

After a period in Britain to validate his US credentials in order to teach in the British system, he returned to Kenya. He was one of the principal architects of the Kikuyu Independent Schools, a school system quite separate from any missionary or colonial connection. In 1939 he founded Kenya Teachers College at Githunguri in the heart of Kikuyuland.

Koinange played a fundamental role in blazing the trail for the numbers of African students who would embark on their educational odyssey two decades later. With the outbreak of the Mau Mau insurgency in 1952, however, the Teachers College was closed. To avoid being picked up and detained like thousands of other Kikuyu, Koinange fled to London where he could actively represent African interests, particularly with the Labour Party. In 1959, he left London when he was invited by Kwame Nkrumah to be Director of East, Central and South Africa in Ghana's Bureau of African Affairs, and in 1960, he moved to Dar es Salaam in Tanganyika to become Secretary-General of the Pan-African Freedom Movement for East, Central, and South Africa (PAFMECA). He returned to Kenya in 1961, about the time that Jomo Kenyatta, the first president of Kenya, was released from detention, where he had been held by the colonial government as the accused leader of the Mau Mau. With the approach of independence, Koinange was elected to Parliament. He served as minister in a number of ministries over the years until his death in 1981 at the age of 74.

During the 1940s and 1950s, teaching was the only professional career an African could aspire to achieve. Two years of training beyond secondary school qualified one to teach in African schools at the primary level. It was a pathway that was heavily travelled. As it had been for Peter Mbiyu Koinange, it became the most important source of emerging African political leadership. When the first election of Africans to the Legislative Council of Kenya (a nascent parliament) took place in 1957, all but one were or had been teachers, including Daniel arap Moi, who later succeeded Jomo Kenyatta as Kenya's second president.

In addition to Peter Mbiyu Koinange, and much to the consternation of the European settlers, a few other Alliance High School graduates created their own opportunities outside of Kenya. Paradoxically, considering the racial situation in South Africa at the time, access to higher education sometimes came from the all-black South African colleges. Fort Hare College in Cape Province (now a university) became the first stop on the road to a degree for several Kenyans. Other Alliance graduates who managed to break out of Kenya in the 1940s succeeded in gaining access to higher education in the United States and Canada.

When these first foreign-educated graduates returned, they were an example and an inspiration to the next generation who, towards the end of the 1950s, would flail in every direction in their consuming desire for higher education.

Chapter 2

A class of notables

Alliance High School class of 1945

The drive for education gained momentum with the Alliance High School class of 1945, which Carey Francis, the English headmaster, called 'a class of notables'. The fifteen students in the class together vowed that, come what may, they would find a way to pursue higher education and earn a degree – somehow, somewhere. It was hard to see how such a rash pledge by African school boys, without resources and thousands of kilometres away from any opportunities, could be carried out. But against all odds, the wishes of twelve of the fifteen prevailed. Seven reached their goal by going to the USA or Canada. The other five went to India or South Africa. Of the three who did not succeed, one was killed during the Mau Mau insurgency, another had a mental breakdown, and the third simply was never able to get out of Kenya.

There were many extraordinary tales of how the twelve succeeded, but one stands out above the others and is integral to this story. In 1956, Julius Gikonyo Kiano of the Alliance class of 1945, was awarded a PhD in Political Science from the University of California, Berkeley. He was the first African from Kenya to attain a doctorate. He achieved this with the price of an air ticket, bought with voluntary contributions from his home area of Murang'a, and the ten dollars in his possession when he landed in the USA. Dr Clark Kerr, Chancellor of the University of California, remarked on a trip to Nairobi in 1959 that he considered Kiano to be the brightest foreign student who had ever attended the university. Some thought there was a bit of hyperbole on Kerr's part, but it was later confirmed by Dr Robert Scalapino, who had been Kiano's academic advisor.

Born in 1926, Kiano grew up in Fort Hall (now Murang'a), eighty kilometres north of Nairobi in Central Province. An extraordinarily fertile area, Murang'a was central to the traditions, culture, and economic life of the Kikuyu and was the heart of Kikuyu resistance to British land settlement and domination. The Mau Mau movement (from the late 1940s to 1960) found many willing adherents there.

Kiano came from a poor family. His father, a farmer, hawked vegetables for a living in Nairobi, where Kiano's uncle was a cook. Some spark in this young man impelled him to seek an education. Though there was little money in the family, with his father's consent, he enrolled in a mission school in Nyeri, forty eight kilometres from his home. To get there, he walked for two days scantily clad and barefoot over goat trails (shoes were a luxury few Africans could afford), subsisting on tea which took the little money he had. He stayed almost continuously at the school as a boarding student because of the difficulty of travelling back and forth. Exceeding all expectations, he passed the exams with high marks and was one of the fortunate few selected in 1942 for a place at Alliance High School.

Eliud Wambu Mathu, one of the earliest Africans to earn a teaching qualification in England, and the only African staff member at Alliance at the time, was the principal teacher.[4] Later to become the first African appointed to the Legislative Council (Kenya's Parliament), Mathu was a hard taskmaster who instilled in his students a strong sense of African identity and an intense desire for higher education. He imbued them with the idea that the only way for them to progress was to obtain further education, and that obtaining it was the only way to win their freedom.

First Kenyan African to earn a PhD

K iano did well at Alliance and after graduating was employed for a time by Peter Mbiyu Koinange as a teacher at Githunguri Teachers College, part of the Kikuyu Independent Schools system that Koinange had helped establish. Kiano had learnt from Koinange about the renowned James Aggrey, the Ghanaian who in 1898 had gone to Livingstone College in North Carolina and later earned a PhD from Columbia University. Aggrey became a legendary educator and intellectual in West Africa, where he was sometimes called the 'Father of African Education' or the 'Booker T Washington of Africa'.

Inspired by the examples of Mathu and Dr Aggrey, Kiano was hungry for further education. The only possibilities at the time were India, Makerere College in Uganda or Fort Hare College in South Africa, then possibly on to the United Kingdom or beyond. Only the senior chiefs (Koinange wa Mbiyu, Josiah Njonjo, Waiyaki wa Hinga) had money to send a son to a place like Fort Hare. Kiano instead accepted one of

---

4　A principal teacher was a promoted post that usually referred to being head of a particular department within a secondary school.

the much-sought-after places at Makerere, offered to only a select few, where a five-year course would give him no degree, but an East African Diploma in Education.[5]

However, Kiano disliked the rigid curriculum at Makerere and the lack of a degree programme – so much so that he was determined to find an alternative. In the Makerere library, he found some old issues of American Negro magazines including *The Crisis*, published by the National Association for the Advancement of Coloured People (NAACP), which carried various advertisements for black schools in the USA. He wrote to several and was accepted by Pioneer Business College in Philadelphia with a full scholarship.

On the strength of this, he quit Makerere in August, 1947, and set about finding funds for transportation and incidentals. His cousin, Muchohi Gikonyo, a well-respected African leader, was at first furious with him for leaving Makerere, but finally agreed to help. He persuaded the Kikuyu Central Association (KCA), an early political organisation, to try to raise the money for an air ticket: 5,000 East African shillings[6] (then about USD$720). A *baraza* (public meeting) was held in Nairobi and brought in close to USD$430, but Kiano was still USD$290 short. A family friend and leading member of KCA, Lewis Waciuma, was so incensed over the failure to raise the full sum that he withdrew his entire savings from a postal account and gave the money to Kiano to meet his goal.

But the roadblocks in Kiano's path were just beginning. The British Director of Education refused to recommend granting him a passport to go to this "second-rate school", and so the colonial government declined to issue it. Kiano, accordingly, got the Vicar from the church in his home area to sign as his sponsor, and the local Native Council of Chiefs passed a resolution calling on the government to issue him a passport. Although this petition was turned down by the District Commissioner, under heavy pressure from many of Kiano's supporters, the government finally relented and issued the passport. The American Consulate, on the strength of Kiano's college acceptance and scholarship, gave him a student visa – until then one of the few that had ever been issued to an African in Kenya.

Small, slight, and bespectacled, Kiano arrived at the airport, ticket in hand, early on a February morning in 1948, booked on a late-morning

---

5 Diplomas were awarded by Makerere. Kiano left Kenya in 1948 and Makerere did not establish any relationship with University College of London until 1949, after which degrees were awarded through the mother institution.

6 EA currency was used in Kenya from 1922-1966. USD are indicated to be specific so that there is no confusion with other dollars.

flight. The passport authorities, however, refused to honour a student visa for an African, and prevented him from leaving. Outraged at such high-handed treatment, some of his friends and supporters sought help from the American Consulate. A visa officer, newly arrived in Nairobi, listened to an irate barrage of Kiswahili of which he understood not a word. He could sense his visitors' frustration, however, and he eventually got the gist of the dilemma. His creative solution was to cancel the student visa and issue in its place a tourist visa, which the airport authorities accepted.

After overcoming hurdles that would have defeated most ordinary mortals, Kiano finally left Kenya in March 1948, bound for the USA with sixty East African shillings (about ten US dollars) in his pocket. The plane was a small one (probably an old DC-3) and flew only in daylight hours on a circuitous route to Khartoum, then Tel Aviv, Rome, and London. By the time Kiano reached London, he had no money left. Fortunately his old mentor, Peter Mbiyu Koinange, was then in London, along with Charles Njonjo, a fellow Kenyan whom Kiano had not met before. Njonjo, who was later to be Kenya's Attorney General, was studying law at the Inns of Court School of Law[7] and came to his aid. He handed over what little money he had with him, and with that and a winter coat of Koinange's, Kiano boarded a plane for New York.

As luck would have it, bad weather forced the plane to land in Boston rather than New York, and Kiano had to travel the rest of the way by bus. He had no idea where Philadelphia was, but when he reached New York, a kind stranger helped him call Pioneer Business College.[8] The person he spoke to at the college gave him directions for getting to Philadelphia, but when he said, "I have no money," the voice on the other end paused, and then told him to stay put and someone would be sent from Philadelphia to fetch him.

On his arrival in Philadelphia with his escort, Kiano learnt that Pioneer College was a business school for secretarial and book keeping courses. It offered no degree. He also learnt that his 'full scholarship' included earning his keep by cleaning the President's quarters and acting as handyman at the school. He worked hard, did his chores, and learnt typing and shorthand between March and August 1948. He realised, though, that he would have to find a different avenue to a degree course, and his luck held. He had struck up a friendship with a black Quaker professor who lived near the school and also knew the president of Storer

7 Now part of The City Law School, City University London.
8 No longer exists.

College[9] in Harpers Ferry, West Virginia. The professor was able to arrange a full scholarship there for Kiano for the 1948-49 academic year.

Still Kiano, after one academic year, was not satisfied that he was in the course of study he most wanted. The people at Storer recognised this after one academic year and were sympathetic. Through the school's contacts, the president's assistant, Mrs Jessie Treichler, helped him get a full scholarship at Antioch College in Ohio. There he found the intellectual challenge he was looking for and the course of study he was after: political science. Incidentally, while at Antioch he also became friends with and dated Coretta Scott, who later married Martin Luther King, Jr.

Kiano graduated with honours from Antioch in 1952 and was accepted for graduate study at Stanford University (fully financed). He blossomed in this environment and in 1953, at the end of his MA programme in Political Science, he was highly recommended by his Stanford professors to Dr Robert Scalapino, a professor of Political Science at the University of California, Berkeley. Within three years Kiano had finished his PhD and had married an African-American woman. He had achieved his educational goals in record time – an extraordinary tribute to the quality of the man, as recognised by his friends and mentors.

When Kiano arrived back in Nairobi with his American wife and child in September 1956, after eight years away, he was not offered employment by the colonial government. In fact, the only job prospect he had was in the private sector as a management trainee with Shell Oil Company. This outraged his cousin Muchohi Gikonyo, who at the time was one of the few appointed African members of the Legislative Council. Muchohi, with a very large physical presence, bullied his way in to see the colonial governor, Sir Evelyn Baring.

"See here," he erupted, "you mean to tell me that the best thing this government has to offer a young man returning here with all that education is a job pumping petrol?"

Evidently the incident had an effect, for not long after that, Kiano was engaged as a lecturer in economics (there being no political science course in the British system) at the Royal Technical College in Nairobi, which was admitting its first students in 1956. The college was the forerunner of the University of Nairobi, though not yet a degree-granting institution. From being a lecturer there, Kiano went on to a long career in

---

9   Storer College was a historically black college located in Harpers Ferry in Jefferson County, West Virginia. It operated from 1865 until 1955. Its former campus is now part of the Harpers Ferry National Historical Park. [Source: Wikipedia]

government after Independence. He was elected to Parliament a number of times, and over the years headed the ministries of Commerce and Industry, Labour, Education, Local Government, and Water Resources. He was also Managing Director of the Industrial Development Bank, Chairman of the Kenya Broadcasting Corporation, and one of Kenya's most respected elder statesmen.

With Kiano's return, and close on his heels the arrival back in Kenya of several others from the USA and the UK, the rush for education overseas was on. Kiano was a hero to his people, a man who had returned from America with the highest honours. In addition to the many high government posts he held over the years, he was an inspiration to students, a touchstone of knowledge, and the ultimate educational counsellor.

First American-educated Kenyan African doctor

Among others of the Alliance class of 1945 who went to the USA in the 1950s were Julius Kariuki Gecau and Mungai Njoroge. Gecau went to a college in India and earned a BA. With the help of the Rev Dr James H Robinson of New York, who later founded a programme called 'Operation Crossroads Africa', Gecau travelled directly to the USA from India. He did not stop in Nairobi because, as he said, "By then, it was the (Mau Mau) Emergency, you know. I couldn't come home. I would have been put in detention."

He said all the students who left had had to take Mau Mau oaths. He himself had taken two. "But apparently the government never found out, and twelve out of our class of fifteen from Alliance High School succeeded in going overseas to college, some to India, some to South Africa, some to the USA."

Sponsored by the Presbyterian Church, Gecau spent a year on an international student lecture tour. He was so impressed by his year of touring and talking to student audiences that thirty years later, he remarked that if his schooling had ended with that experience, he would still have had an invaluable education. He had, however, been fortunate enough to follow up on his year of touring with a scholarship at the University of Chicago, where he received his Master's degree in Economics. One of the professors whom he remembered best was economist George Pratt Schultz, who later became President Reagan's Secretary of State from 1982 to 1989. Upon completion of his degree, Gecau immediately returned to Kenya. He went to work for the British

American Tobacco Company (BAT), where he was personnel manager, and later was appointed Managing Director of Kenya Power and Lighting Company.

Mungai Njoroge, Kenya's first American-educated physician went from South Africa's Fort Hare College in 1951 to Stanford University to study medicine. Prior to his return to Kenya in 1958, Dr Njoroge was the featured personality on the television show, 'This Is Your Life', hosted by Ralph Edwards. His parents and sister were flown from Kenya for the show, joining American friends who had been helpful in Mungai's educational career.

British colonial authorities refused to recognise his American medical degree and, he was forced to go to Canada to take board examinations that would enable him to practice in Kenya. Upon his return home, he made fruitless attempts to rent space for a clinic from landlords suspicious of an American-educated African doctor. Finally, accompanied by myself, a white American to vouch for him, he convinced a local businessman to rent to him space. He was then able to open a clinic in Thika Town, about thirty two kilometres from Nairobi.

After Kenya's independence in 1963, Dr Njoroge (later known as Dr Mungai), left his practice to become not only President Kenyatta's personal physician but also Minister for Health. He later led the ministries of Defence, Foreign Affairs, and Environment and Natural Resources.

Chapter 3

From small beginnings

A trickle grows

As far as could be determined, between 1949 and Dr Kiano's return in 1956, only about twenty five Kenyan students trickled out to India, South Africa, Britain, or the USA. Exactly how many is difficult to say, since during those years few records were kept.

One of those who went to India was Mugo Gatheru, a close friend of Kiano's. He grew up in the Rift Valley where his father worked as a squatter on a European farm, and later went to a mission school near Fort Hall (Murang'a). After completing secondary school, he worked for a while as a laboratory technician in a government laboratory in Nairobi. There he witnessed firsthand the discriminatory practices against Africans and Asians and began sending letters and articles critical of the government to the settler-friendly *Kenya Weekly News*. The eyes of the government and the Criminal Investigation Department (CID) were already on him when he was asked by Jomo Kenyatta to become assistant editor of *The African Voice*, the official newspaper of the Kenya African Union (KAU), an early African political party, which was headed by Kenyatta. Gatheru resigned from the government laboratory job in 1947 and began writing articles for *The African Voice* in which he continued to protest against the 'pass laws', the colour bar, and the poor wages and living conditions of Africans.

Meanwhile, with the examples of Peter Mbiyu Koinange and Gikonyo Kiano in mind, he began to pursue a dream of obtaining a higher education. He wrote to the American Consul in Nairobi requesting the names of Negro[10] newspapers, magazines, and colleges in the USA, and received several. Already a budding writer whose autobiography would one day be published along with a scholarly work on Kenya's history, he began writing letters to American colleges and sending articles to the *Associated Negro Press* in Chicago. One of his letters caught the attention of St Clair Drake, a well-known Africanist and a professor at Roosevelt University in Chicago. With Drake's help, Gatheru was

---

10 'Negro' was the term used in the 1940s-1950s. Black was the term used in the 1960s. Later the term became African-American.

offered a scholarship to study at Roosevelt University. Unfortunately he couldn't accept it. Labelled a 'subversive' for his public criticism of the colonial government, he was denied the necessary papers to go to the USA. However, after writing a non-stop blitz of letters to everyone from the Colonial Office and the Governor of Kenya to other junior officers, he was finally granted a visa to go to India instead.

Many people contributed money to enable him to go. Friends and family held tea parties, his father sold land, and he received additional help from a wealthy Arab businessman[11] in Nairobi who owned a restaurant. In 1949 he left for college in India. While there, he maintained his correspondence with Professor Drake, who assured him his scholarship was still available if he could make his way to Roosevelt University. With help from an uncle back in Kenya and from some American Negro churches, Gatheru raised the money for his air ticket, and arrived in Chicago in the spring of 1950.

Unfortunately, by the time he got there, he found that his scholarship had been cancelled. Instead, Professor Drake negotiated a small scholarship to cover three summer courses at Roosevelt University, and then helped Gatheru get a scholarship to Bethune-Cookman University, a small black college in Florida. From there he went to Lincoln University in Pennsylvania, then on to New York University for graduate work. While in New York he married a white American woman, Dolores Pienkowski. Upon completing his master's degree, he went to London for a law degree, assisted this time by William Scheinman, a wealthy American businessman who had helped many other African students.

Mugo Gatheru: A Child-of-Two Worlds

In his autobiography, *A Child-of-Two Worlds,* Gatheru described his odyssey from an isolated rural peasant culture to a highly developed and largely urban one. The book is a fascinating psychological study of the dislocation he experienced in coping with two drastically different cultures. As he states in the book, "Never at any time did I lose my identity as a Kenyan, but ... after a while I ... caught myself reacting like an American."

In 1969 Gatheru accepted a teaching position at California State University in Sacramento, where he taught African and Middle Eastern History until his retirement in 2002.

---

11 Gatheru does not name him in his book, *A Child-of-Two Worlds*, nor when interviewed. He described him as "a wealthy Arab restaurant owner".

For all of those aspiring Africans who tried to go to the USA before 1957, the obstacles were many and daunting, as illustrated by the experiences of Gatheru and Kiano. Despite rising American public interest in Africa, the official United States Government response to the need for more educational opportunities and more scholarships was mired in their own bureaucracy. A United States Information Service (USIS) office in Nairobi was just getting off the ground in late 1955, and the Cultural Affairs office in USIS, with almost no resources, was barely in existence by mid-1956. Consequently, there was limited contact between Americans in the Consulate and Africans. Almost no information on American schools was available in Nairobi, applications were difficult to obtain, and USA schools lacked the means to evaluate applicants.

As previously noted, settlers and colonial government officials, with few exceptions, had no interest in assisting in the higher education of Africans. More often they were downright antagonistic to the idea, fearing the threat to presumed white supremacy inherent in the prospect of an educated African population. But despite the lack of information and contact with Americans and the opposition of Europeans, some students seeking higher education continued to leave.

Three schools in the USA seemed particularly interested in accepting students from Kenya. Central State College in Ohio and Lincoln University in Pennsylvania were both black schools, with Lincoln becoming the training ground for a number of later African leaders. The third, Ohio Wesleyan University, gave scholarships to one or two Kenyans each year from about 1952 on, likely due to Peter Mbiyu Koinange's attendance there in the early 1930s.

The earliest of those at Ohio Wesleyan who could be traced was Ng'ang'a Mwenja. He arrived at the college in 1955 after a journey that for perils and thrills rivalled that of Dr Kiano – seven years earlier. Mwenja succeeded in becoming an engineer and returned well before Independence to a position in the Nairobi City Government. He later rose to become the chief engineer of the city's water system and ensured a supply of safe and drinkable water – one of the few in Africa.

Many others went early

An early arrival (1953) at Lincoln University was Kariuki Njiiri. Kariuki's father, Senior Chief Njiiri wa Karanja was a respected senior chief of the Kikuyu and was honoured by Queen Elizabeth II for his loyal service during the Mau Mau insurrection. Chief Njiiri reportedly had forty two wives and over a hundred children, of whom Kariuki was the only one to achieve a college education. He did well at primary school and his father found the means to send him to high school in Bombay, India. There he met the Rev Dr James H Robinson, pastor of the Presbyterian Church of the Master in New York City – the same Rev Robinson who had helped Julius Gecau get to the USA. Robinson saw the potential in this young Kenyan and arranged his admission, along with some scholarship assistance, to Lincoln University, Rev Robinson's alma mater. After completing a BA at Lincoln, Njiiri went on to the New School of Social Research (now the New School University) in New York City, where he received a Master's degree in Sociology and Anthropology. He returned to Kenya in 1958 with an American wife whom he had met while she was working as Rev Robinson's personal secretary. From 1958 on, these American wives, Earnestine Kiano and Ruth Njiiri, were instrumental in helping Kenyans get to the United States and in finding living arrangements and family sponsors for some, especially the young women who had been unable to finish secondary school in Kenya and hence were bound for American high schools.

Another early bird at Lincoln, there at the same time as Kariuki Njiiri, was Samuel Ayodo, who had come on one of the first Fulbright travel grants awarded to a Kenyan. Ayodo earned his degree from Lincoln and returned to Kenya before Njiiri. He later became a Member of the Legislative Council and one of the first ministers in President Jomo Kenyatta's cabinet when self-government was attained.

Others in the early vanguard to the USA, all of whom left on their own initiative, made their way via India like Kariuki Njiiri. Josephat Njuguna Karanja graduated from college in India and won a graduate fellowship to study history at Princeton University. Dr Karanja went on to become Vice President of Kenya from 1988-89. Dr Mungai Njoroge's two brothers, Ngethe Mu Njoroge and Nyoike Njoroge, were part of this early group also. One went to Central State College in Ohio and later to Temple University, while the other attended Boston University. Both obtained degrees and returned home sometime after their brother Mungai.

Before 1955, there had been no USA government involvement in higher education for Africans, but beginning that year, ever so slowly and in hit-or-miss fashion, some American government scholarships began filtering through the Institute of International Education (IIE) in New York. Of those who were assisted in this way, several were Indian and three were ethnic Poles whose families fled Poland at the beginning of World War II. None were Africans.

In 1956, two Africans received scholarships: Shadrack N Okova graduated from Columbia University, became a Member of Parliament, and later went into business. Hezekiah Openda attended the University of Chicago on a Fulbright scholarship. After graduating, he began a teaching career and eventually became assistant director of civil aviation and the first Kenyan principal of the East African School of Aviation in the Ministry of Transport and Communication. He retired from government service in 1992 and was ordained an Anglican priest in 1993. He died in 2005.

From the group of about twenty five students who went to the USA between 1949 and 1956, the three Poles and one or two Indians never returned home. Two Africans also stayed in the USA. Both were Kikuyu and had been politically active at home. With the Mau Mau Emergency still ongoing when they obtained their degrees, they would have risked being detained indefinitely by the colonial authorities had they come back to Kenya.

1957 – The first official USA Government programme in Kenya begins

An official USA government programme, administered by Dr Jack Mower, Cultural Affairs Officer at USIS, began in Kenya in July, 1957, before my arrival in Nairobi. Seven Smith-Mundt grants and IIE scholarships from private sources were awarded, pieced out with Fulbright travel grants. Five went to Africans, one to a Pole and one to an Indian. The five Africans included John Cheruiyot, Reuben Muilu, Hilary Ng'weno, Nicholas Otieno, and Lawrence Sagini.

Nicholas Otieno, who had earned a BA in England by 1956, was only the third African from Kenya to have received a degree. He returned to Kenya to teach at Alliance High School. In 1957 he won a graduate fellowship in Botany at Cornell University. After obtaining a PhD, he came back to Kenya and founded the Botany Department at the Royal Technical College of East Africa (now University of Nairobi) and to become its chairman.

Lawrence Sagini received a full scholarship to Allegheny College in Pennsylvania. He was born in 1927 and had grown up in Kisii, a highland area near Lake Victoria and the major tea producer of Kenya. Sagini remembered reading in intermediate school in the 1930s about Dr James Aggrey and his statement that "when you educate a man, you educate a man, but when you educate a woman you educate a whole family". It was a revolutionary concept in Africa at the time but it was a truism that stuck in Sagini's mind. He said that later, in 1962 as a Member of

Parliament for Kitutu and Minister for Education, he was influenced by this philosophy when trying to provide more schooling for women.

Sagini knew of several Kenyan Africans who, like Peter Mbiyu Koinange, had gone overseas for further education, and he was determined to do the same. However, when he left secondary school in 1948, he took the only avenue open to him, which was Kagumo Training College in Nyeri. He then taught at a school in his home area of Kisii from 1949 to 1953. For an additional four years, until 1957, he was headmaster of a mission school in Nyanza.

During that time he met an American anthropologist, Dr Robert LeVine, from Loyola University in New Orleans, who was doing research in Kisii. Dr LeVine tried unsuccessfully to help Sagini gain admittance to various Jesuit schools in the USA, and encouraged him to apply to other colleges, among them Allegheny College in Pennsylvania. Allegheny officials, at first troubled by his lack of certain qualifications, were nevertheless so impressed by his application, his articulateness, and Dr LeVine's recommendation, that they awarded him a special scholarship. At Allegheny, he worked straight through the summers to complete a BA degree in Sociology in just two years. He returned to Kenya in 1959.

One of the first things he did when he arrived back in Nairobi was to seek me out at USIS to tell me what a superb experience he had had at Allegheny, and how well he had been treated. He extolled the virtues of American education and said, "If there is ever anything I can do for America, please let me know."

It was clear that Allegheny's regard for him was equally high; in 1969 he was awarded an honorary degree of Doctor of Laws and was invited to be the Commencement Speaker that year. He served in Kenya's Parliament for a number of years, was Minister for Education and also Minister for Natural Resources in President Kenyatta's first cabinet.

Hilary Boniface Ng'weno was the recipient of a most unusual full scholarship to Harvard in nuclear physics. He was considered by his peers to be the most brilliant student ever to have attended Mang'u High School. His schoolmate, Joe Wanjui, described him as "a genius, a brain machine. He could have achieved (success) in any field."

Ng'weno was also something of a young political radical, and he was not happy at Harvard. At the end of the first year, he packed his bags and went to the Soviet Union. It was not long, however, before he became disillusioned by his experience there. The following year he returned to Harvard to pick up from where he had left off. He graduated with a BSc degree and returned to Kenya in 1962, where for many years he established himself as a career editor. In 1975, he founded *The Weekly Review*, a journal of political news, commentary and analysis that was often critical of the government. He is also an author of a number of books and is revered for his TV productions in the series *Makers of a Nation* covering Kenya's post-independent political history.

Of the remaining two, John Cheruiyot studied Civil Engineering at the University of Colorado, and Reuben Muilu majored in Economics at Indiana University.

The trickle becomes a river

By 1958, the Africans' clamour for higher education had become more insistent. When I arrived in Nairobi as Cultural Affairs Officer in November, 1957, Dr Mower at USIS had begun to acquire a library of college catalogues and other educational references. Throughout 1958 and 1959, my office became the point of contact for assistance and direction, and the long lines of applicants and information seekers became the daily norm outside my office door.

At the same time, American interest in Africa was growing. From 1957 on, various USA educators informed themselves through visits to East Africa. Among them were university presidents such as Clark Kerr from the University of California at Berkeley, Father Theodore Hesburgh from Notre Dame, and others from Earlham College, Brandeis University, and Western College for Women, and so on.

Clearly there was a fast-rising tide of demands for higher education, but still official USA Government scholarships for Kenyan Africans would increase from five in 1957 to only nine in 1958, and that only after constant entreaties and a flood of dispatches to Washington from the Consulate in Nairobi. Even with these few scholarships, there were frustrating problems. Washington insisted that candidates possess a qualification of two years beyond high school, something not required of American students for college entrance. It was difficult to convince officials in Washington or New York that because of the lack of educational institutions in East Africa, there were almost no Africans with such qualifications, and that the requirement should be relaxed. Until 1958 it was often European or Asian candidates who were selected. The ethnic Poles referred to earlier were chosen simply because they could meet the requirement. The question became: For whom were these scholarships intended?

At the heart of the problem was the fact that the official Fulbright and Smith-Mundt programmes, sponsored and paid for by the American taxpayer, were originally geared to Europe and other areas whose populations had reached higher educational levels. For instance, the Fulbright Commission in London acted as the selection body for Fulbright grants to all colonies or territories under the British flag. Not only was that inconvenient but at times it was discriminatory. It totally ignored Kenyan realities and left out of the process the presumably better-informed American consular representatives on the scene.

The USA government and its agent, the Institute of International Education (IIE), seemed unable to respond quickly or creatively to a compelling need in this fast-changing part of Africa. It was only after considerable effort by the Cultural Affairs Office and the USA Consulate in Nairobi that waivers from the State Department were finally obtained in 1959 to allow the selection of students who possessed only a high school certificate.

In the meantime, opposition continued from the colonial government and the white settlers to higher education for all but a chosen few Africans, especially to higher education in America. The prevailing attitude was expressed by Carey Francis, the headmaster of the prestigious Alliance High School. He was cautiously willing to 'allow' a few of the very best to go to select institutions in Britain – i.e., Cambridge, Oxford, or St. Andrews. But as he stated at every opportunity, he had a low opinion of education in America and India and strongly opposed African students going to either. He believed that "... the frenzied thirst for and confidence in overseas education was a major difficulty for Kenya ... To many, the nature of the course was immaterial so long as it was a course, and one course led, not to work, but to yet another course." He went on to say, "Most (Africans) were leaving important work for unsuitable courses in India and, to a lesser extent, in the USA ..." He feared that "... in a few years time, many would return disillusioned and embittered, unfitted for any useful work, with fourth-rate degrees from fifth-rate universities."

In one sense, Francis was prophetic. Although students did not return from the USA "disillusioned and embittered" with their education, many of the first returnees *became* embittered towards the colonial government when they were offered little in the way of employment. The Colonial Office in London often reserved posts in Kenya for career officers displaced from areas no longer in the Empire (i.e., India and Malaysia), at the expense of returning Kenyans with overseas degrees.

People like Dr Kiano, with first-rate degrees from first-rate universities, were passed over in favour of white expatriate officers. This policy led to much friction between the colonial government and a growing group of well-educated African leaders. After increasing protests, some posts were gained, but the issue would not be fully resolved until the advent of Kenyan Independence in December 1963.

1958 – Full USA Government scholarships awarded to Africans

Not until 1958 were several Africans selected for full USA government scholarships. That year, six scholarships out of a total of nine went to Africans: Francis Kanyua, Albert Maleche, James Maina Wanjigi, Simon Mbae, Nehemia Othieno, and Daniel Owino. The mix finally reflected a distribution closer to the actual demographics of Kenya: six Africans, one Goan, one Indian, and one young man from a white settler family. Several had credentials roughly equivalent to a baccalaureate degree.[12] Their selection was based partially on an estimate of their ability to perform in an American academic environment. All six Africans subsequently received Master's degrees and Maleche went on to attain a PhD, as did two of the three non-Africans: David Hopcraft and Mangat Jagjit Singh.

Francis Kanyua received a BA degree from Depaw University and an MA degree in Economics from Indiana University. He was recruited in 1962 by a Kenya manpower team canvassing the USA for Kenyan graduates. By then, everyone recognised that Kenya would very soon be independent from Britain, and the rush to find educated personnel was on. Kanyua, who had studied at the Royal Technical College (now University of Nairobi) under Dr Kiano, worked first at the Ministry of Finance, and then transferred to the Ministry of Commerce and Industry when Kiano became its Minister. He was later the Executive Officer of the Kenya Export Promotion Council (KEPC). It was, he said, "the greatest job I ever had." One of the things that made it so was the opportunity to travel the globe extensively, learning things that could be incorporated into the management of Kenya's foreign trade. He subsequently became the Director of Industries for the Ministry of Commerce and Industry. Finally, after several other responsible positions, he was the logical choice to become the Executive Director of the Kenya Chamber of Commerce.

---

12 An academic degree conferred by a college or university upon those who complete the undergraduate curriculum.

James Maina Wanjigi was difficult to locate for an interview, since he changed his name to Maina Wanjigi when he returned to Kenya. This was not at all unusual. A common practice was to give a child the grandparent's name – a single name only, there being traditionally no general family name. Thus a son might be named Gikonyo after his grandfather, but answer to Gikonyo wa Kuria, or son of Kuria – not unlike Johnson, the son of John, in the Western world. A Christian name might be added, and Gikonyo wa Kuria might then be Lucas Gikonyo, or Lucas Gikonyo Kuria. After independence, in the Africanising process, the Christian name was sometimes dropped and the person might then call himself Gikonyo Kuria or, for not very clear reasons, Kuria Gikonyo. Dr Mungai Njoroge was one who later reversed his name and became known as Dr Njoroge Mungai. Such name switching made it difficult to know whom you were looking for, which demonstrates why finding the former students was occasionally such a challenge.

Maina Wanjigi had a Diploma of Education in agriculture from Makerere College and at the time of his application for the USA government scholarship was working as an assistant agricultural officer in Murang'a. Dr Kiano had encouraged him to apply and sent him to me at the Cultural Affairs Office. It was obvious, when I interviewed him, that he was well qualified. Upon learning that he had been selected, he asked his superiors in the Ministry of Agriculture for a leave of absence in order to accept, in his words, "this prestigious scholarship." He was refused leave and in answer he resigned and left anyway.

He earned a BSc degree in Agriculture from the University of Connecticut in one year, then was offered a Rockefeller Foundation Fellowship that enabled him to attend Stanford University for a MSc degree in Applied Agricultural Economics. At Stanford, he worked with the World Trade Institute and with the Food Research Institute that conducted fieldwork, education, and research on agriculture and food issues in developing countries in Africa, Asia, and Latin America. He returned to Kenya in 1961 and later remarked that the courses he had taken in the USA were immediately applicable to the situation at home. In his words, "It was a wonderful experience and could not have been better in any way."

With his first-class degree in agricultural economics from a topflight university, he went to see the Establishments (Personnel) Officer for the colonial government. He described the meeting as the biggest joke he had heard since coming home. He was told that he was "overqualified" and that there was no job for him in the Ministry of Agriculture in Nairobi. It should be emphasised that in 1961, the white settlers still exercised total control over all cash crops in Kenya, and Africans were not allowed to participate in that economy. Only small-scale subsistence agriculture was the Africans' lot.

Failing anything else, Wanjigi took the only job available, a low-level position as an agricultural officer in an African area. The pay was the equivalent of USD$2,057 per year. Colleagues with whom he had worked prior to going to the USA were now at much higher levels than him. However, when the political situation began to change in 1962, he was instrumental in introducing African farmers to cash crop farming: planting coffee, tea, pyrethrum, cotton and raising dairy herds. This enabled Africans to move quickly into a cash market economy and boosted their standard of living beyond their fondest dreams. It was not long before the quality of their crops and cattle out-distanced those of the settlers, and African farmers were walking away with prizes at the many annual agricultural fairs. When Kenya became independent, Wanjigi was appointed as a minister in President Kenyatta's cabinet.

Of the other Africans on USA government scholarships in 1958, Daniel Owino finished a Master's degree at Ohio State University, joined Kenya's Foreign Service, and became an ambassador and also a minister in President Kenyatta's government.

Albert Maleche received his PhD in Educational Psychology and became a professor at the University of Nairobi.

Nehemiah Othieno graduated from Columbia Teachers College after majoring in Education, and also returned to Kenya to become a university professor.

The sixth member of this group, Daniel Mbae, received a degree in Zoology from New York University. After returning home, he served as a Member of Parliament from Meru, but unfortunately died soon after.

David Hopcraft, the most unusual official grantee

David Hopcraft was the only recipient of a United States Government scholarship who came from a long-established white settler family and who had a background in British public (read private) school education. His grandfather had fought in the Boer War in South Africa and later immigrated to Kenya, where he fell in love with the country and never left. David's father owned land in several parts of Kenya, including a farm in Njoro in the White Highlands where David was born.

From the age of five, David was sent to a series of boarding schools, but he was a rebel and "... never lasted long at any of them." Growing up, he had never felt truly part of the settler culture; he had played mostly with African boys and learnt to speak both Kiswahili and Kikuyu. He finally graduated with a Cambridge School Certificate at the age of eighteen, and then got his Higher School Certificate at a London school. He enrolled briefly at the University of London, but did not stay long there either. Back in Kenya he was casting around for something to do when his sister encouraged him to enter the USA scholarship competition. David decided that a USA education could not be any worse than what he had already experienced, so although he believed his chances were "less than zero", he applied.

He was the only young man from a settler family ever to apply. He was well qualified with his Higher School Certificate, so after intense questioning by the USA Scholarship Committee, to his great surprise he was chosen. The Institute of International Education (IIE) placed him at Berea College in Kentucky, an odd choice given that Berea at the time was a self-help college mainly devoted to agriculture and trade for students from Appalachia. The curriculum included work on vocational projects and on the college farm.

Berea had high standards, and in spite of the fact that he was more worldly and mature than most students there, David loved the people and was happy in the school's friendly, informal atmosphere. Berea was also a place where David could build his own course of study, which gave him a freedom he had been denied in the British system. With two years' credit for his Higher School Certificate, he completed a BA degree in two years.

He was awarded a United Nations scholarship to attend any school in the world, and he chose Cornell, where he received a Master's degree and a PhD. His thesis was on wildlife management, using Kenya as his laboratory. On his father's land thirty two kilometres southeast of Nairobi he began a long, rigorously controlled study of the relative effects of wildlife on the environment as compared with those of domesticated animals. The outcome was clear evidence that game herds do not damage the land or soil, but actually improve it. Cattle, goats and sheep, on the other hand, impact the earth and eat all the vegetation indiscriminately, leaving the land more arid and considerably less profitable.

David received permission from the Kenya government to raise gazelles, impala, hartebeest, and various other game as sources of meat for local restaurants like the Carnivore, on the edge of the Nairobi Game Park (Nairobi National Park). He has been associated with a number of environmental groups and has given many major presentations around the world detailing the results of his research.

Those who left privately in 1958

Of the thirty one students who made their own arduous arrangements and raised the necessary funds in 1958, one young man stands out as most remarkable. Sometime in May, 1958, Joseph Barage Wanjui appeared at the Cultural Affairs Office, which at the time was located on the second floor of an old building overlooking the outdoor Nairobi City Market. This was primarily an African produce and handicraft market and often the traffic noise and hawkers' cries made conversation in my office a challenging proposition.

Wanjui had received a First Class Cambridge School Certificate and was working as a senior clerk in a company in Nairobi. In high school, he had achieved a distinction in science. This, coupled with his First Class Cambridge School Certificate, assured his acceptance at Makerere College with all expenses paid for a course leading to a medical degree. (Makerere had in 1953 began awarding a handful of external degrees from University College of London). Wanjui was determined, however, to go to the USA and had been accepted at Ohio Wesleyan for the fall term with a scholarship covering tuition, room and board but not transport.

After a lengthy conversation with me in my office and a weekend spent wrestling with his decision, Wanjui decided in favour of Ohio Wesleyan. Though he was offered a Fulbright travel grant through a personal contact I had in the Fulbright Commission in London, he accepted instead one from the African-American Institute. Wanjui was on his way.

He did exceptionally well at Wesleyan and went on for a Master's degree in Industrial Engineering at Columbia University, an unusual course for a Kenyan African at the time. By the time he graduated in 1964, Kenya was independent, but he had no idea how he would be able to use his qualifications in an industrial/commercial setting still dominated by the British and Indians. As it turned out, he need not have worried. He was almost immediately snapped up by the Kenya government to head the Industrial and Commercial Development Corporation (ICDC). He went on from there to become one of Kenya's most prominent and influential businessmen and eventually Chancellor of the University of Nairobi.

Certainly the careful selection process, based strictly on merit, was one element in the remarkable success of the 1958 group – and later the one in 1959. But the real credit must be given to the individuals involved: their drive, discipline, patience, work ethic, willingness to take responsibility, and the extent to which they made the most of every opportunity.

Finally, one additional factor contributed to the success of these two groups: timing. They all returned to Kenya during the years either immediately before or just after independence, when the need was greatest and the opportunity existed for rapid advancement in a new African government and society.

Chapter 4

Prelude to the first Airlift

In 1957, approximately thirty nine Kenyans were studying at colleges and universities in the United States, ranging from Alcorn Agricultural and Mechanical College in Mississippi and Hawkins College in Texas to Stanford and Harvard Universities. The numbers increased in 1958, though not remarkably, as small waves of bright young Kenyans began arriving on America's shores. Like their predecessors, they were dropped into an unfamiliar world, a technologically advanced civilisation for which they had little preparation. They were faced by a sink-swim proposition, a challenge that in itself would prove to be an education of significant proportions.

On that side of the Atlantic, colleges and universities became particularly interested in the social and educational blossoming of these young Africans. Their interest was the result not only of their greater awareness of Africa, but also of a genuine desire to help in the educational development of an area that badly needed attention before the political situation got out of control. Many were also intrigued by the prospect of students coming from a little-known part of the globe and by the cross-cultural infusion that might result. Similar interest was already being shown by private American groups, especially foundations, churches, labour unions and others.

As the Mau Mau Emergency wound down, the colonial government and many whites remained hostile to any contacts between Africans and whites, which continued to be monitored. However, in 1957 a shift in American diplomatic personnel brought more frequent and broader engagements with the African community. This sometimes made for tense relations between Americans, colonials, and settlers. But greater American contact with rising young African leaders gradually became more accepted, especially after the first eight Africans were elected to the Legislative Council in 1957.

A labour leader and rising young African politician

Impetus to the growing tide of students stemmed from the interaction of a few Americans with a small group of young Kenyan leaders. One of the Kenyans, Thomas Joseph Mboya, in particular captured the imagination of many Americans. Among the most charismatic political leaders that Kenya ever produced, he was just twenty six years old when he first visited the United States in 1956. During his visit he garnered numerous scholarship offers, charmed American and Canadian philanthropists, and secured cooperation and funds from even the most reluctant of sources.

Mboya was a Luo (Suba), a tribe clustered on the shores of Lake Victoria, four hundred and eighty three kilometres West of Nairobi, but he was born and spent his early years among the Kikuyu and the Akamba near Kitui, Northeast of Nairobi, where his father worked on a sisal plantation.

He first attended a Catholic mission school in Kamba territory. Later, in 1942, at the age of twelve he went to boarding school in his 'home' district near Lake Victoria, an area he was seeing for the first time. The priests there recommended him to the Holy Ghost College at Mang'u, Kenya's second African high school, close to where he had been born but in Kikuyuland.

Mboya's schooling in three different tribal areas gave him a broader, less tribalised outlook than that of most Africans. He was good at languages and fluent in Kamba, Kikuyu, Luo, Kiswahili, and English, which gained him a better understanding of other cultures and reinforced his non-ethnic perspective.

After Mboya's first two years at Mang'u, his father – worn out from the hard work on the sisal plantation – returned to the family's home village on Rusinga Island in Lake Victoria. There was no money for Tom to continue in school, though he had passed the examination to do so. Casting about, he found a course at the Royal Sanitary Institute (now Kenya Institute of Administration) in Nairobi. It not only allowed him to continue his education, but provided a cash stipend. He no longer had to draw upon the family for support and was also able to help pay the school fees for a younger brother, Alphonce Okuku. The sanitary course resulted in his qualifying as a sanitary inspector in Nairobi, in 1950. It was an inauspicious beginning, perhaps, but it was destined to determine his future, making cosmopolitan Nairobi his permanent home and giving him the secure political base he would need for the changes to come.

As David Goldsworthy states in his book, *Tom Mboya: The Man Kenya Wanted To Forget* (1982); "The city was his natural environment. He was wholly at home in its secular, multi-tribal atmosphere ... (and) discovered in himself, almost overnight, a keen sense of the political ... (H)e was not yet a man on the political platform. But he was already a politicised man."

His job soon led him into a long involvement in trade unionism when he began organising the Nairobi African Local Government

Servants Association (NALGSA) and shortly thereafter the Kenya Local Government Workers Union (KLGWU) government staff into, first, an association and shortly thereafter, a union. This was bitterly opposed by both the white settlers and the Kenya colonial government, but with a Labour government in power in Britain in 1951, a move to quash such activity was blunted.

With the advent of the Mau Mau Emergency in 1952 and the incarceration of many of the Kikuyu leaders of the Kenya African Union (KAU) – a political, not a trade, union – Mboya joined KAU and made the leap into the political arena. He never left.

His trade union activities had brought him recognition, not only from the Labour movement in Britain, but from the influential International Confederation of Free Trade Unions (ICFTU). Mboya was being viewed as *the* rising African union leader on the continent. The *New York Times* in October 1955 picked up the theme in an article, *African Leader Looms in Kenya*. As a result of so much attention, he was sponsored by the Fabian Society[13] and the Trade Union Congress in England for a year at Ruskin College of Oxford University.

Though supremely self-confident, Mboya had long been frustrated by not having completed his formal education. Ruskin was ideal for him. Since he was held to no formal course structure, he was able to concentrate on the subjects important to him – economics, political science, and industrial relations. In his own words, "The year at Oxford gave me more confidence in myself; it gave me the time to read more, it taught me to look to books as a source of knowledge. It led me to take part in intellectual discussions, sometimes of a very provocative nature, and it helped me to think more analytically about problems and work out on paper how best to meet them."[14] He was now prepared for what lay ahead.

To many, Mboya was a puzzle – "a riddle wrapped in a mystery inside an enigma," to borrow a phrase from Winston Churchill. Brilliant, impressively poised for one so young, awed by nothing and later by no one, and with no apparent consciousness of race, he was articulate, witty, charming, and enjoyable to be with. He was also dedicated to a democratic ideal and had a messianic commitment to the goal of African independence, yet he was pragmatic in his approach. A spellbinding orator, he could hold an African crowd or a European university assemblage enthralled, often speaking extemporaneously, without notes.

---

13 The Fabian Society is a British socialist organisation whose purpose is to advance the principles of socialism via gradualist and reformist, rather than revolutionary, means.

14 *Freedom and After* by Tom Mboya, Page 38.

At the same time, he could be crafty, secretive, and imperious, always in control of the situation. In conversation he was constantly watchful, on guard. Goldsworthy pictures him as "... not a man for close friendships. Charming, smiling, and casual one moment, he could be preoccupied, impassive, and aloof the next. Seldom ... did Tom Mboya stop thinking, calculating, planning." And yet he had a long memory and often expressed sincere gratitude for another's kindness or assistance.

At the conclusion of his year at Ruskin, he was invited to visit the United States with the joint sponsorship of the American Committee on Africa (ACOA) and The American Federation of Labour and Congress of Industrial Organisations (AFL–CIO). He arrived in New York on 15 August 1956, his 26th birthday. It was there that Mboya first met Frank Montero and William Scheinman of the ACOA. Scheinman committed himself to raising funds, often from his own resources, to help young Kenyans who had scholarships to USA colleges but no money for transport. He was further involved in this effort when he visited Kenya in 1957 and toured the country with Mboya and myself.

African-American Students Foundation

In the spring of 1959, when Mboya visited the United States again, he met the movers and shakers – people like Vice President Richard Nixon, Senator John F Kennedy, Adlai Stevenson, Senator Humphrey, and a host of others across the USA. He was covered in newspaper articles and appeared on "Meet The Press," spoke at colleges and universities, and garnered a significant number of scholarships and other contributions, rapidly outstripping Scheinman's ability to finance transport for so many. Before Mboya returned to Kenya in May 1959, he and Scheinman formed the African-American Students Foundation (AASF), with Scheinman as President. Its goal was to raise travel funds for a 'student airlift' – an idea that had been germinating since their first meeting in 1956.

The other board members were Frank Montero, Theodore W Kheel, President of the National Urban League, Dr Buell M Gallagher, President of City College of New York, Jackie Robinson, former baseball star and a *New York Post* columnist, Mrs Ralph Bunche, Mrs Cora Weiss, Julius Nyerere, later Prime Minister for Tanganyika, and Tom Mboya. A fund-raising committee consisting of well-known black Americans; Harry Belafonte, Sidney Poitier, and Jackie Robinson collected more than USD$35,000 from some 8,000 contributors. As Goldsworthy notes, "Mboya's dream of a 'student airlift' was about to become a reality."

First East African student Airlift, 1959: Preparations

In June, 1959, Mboya was back in Kenya, beginning the final preparations for the 'student airlift'. With financing assured from the USA, a Britannia aircraft with eighty one seats was chartered. But the challenges were many. It had to be determined who the best-qualified candidates were, who had a college admission and other support, and who had all the necessary papers in order to board the aircraft. Not a simple task, given the limited time of just two and a half months available before the start of the school year.

The selection committee consisted of Tom Mboya, Dr Kiano, Kariuki Njiiri, and myself. With the other three each lobbying for their own favourite candidates, I found myself in the role of a mediator. But in the end it was agreed that all candidates would be screened by the whole committee and selections would be based on academic merit alone.

At one point during those hectic days, it became clear that the number of scholarships awarded by the selection committee fell short of the number needed to fill the eighty-one seats on the aircraft. Other students, therefore, who had made their own arrangements to study in the United States but lacked transport, were selected to fill the plane.

The excitement was palpable as the time drew near, in early September, for the plane to take off. At times, it approached a frenzy, especially for the USA Visa Officer, for myself, for the students and their relatives, and for the African leaders tying down scholarships and raising last minute funds. By flight time on 7 September 1959, the eighty-one seats were filled and double-checked. The first East African Airlift was about to begin.

The colonial authorities were nervous and there was a heavy police presence at the airport that night. However, despite the fact that the African crowd of friends and relatives exceeded five thousand, there were no disturbances. Instead, a jubilant, festive atmosphere prevailed. It was without a doubt a high point in the lives of all the Africans there, an event without parallel. There were few corners or dusty back roads in Kenya where people were not caught up in the excitement of this dramatic flight of eighty one of their boys and girls to far-away America to go to college. The goodwill created for the USA and Canada was immense. Evidence of this remained strong for more than a generation, as attested by the many Airlifters who sent their own children to be educated in the USA and Canada.

Chapter 5

The First East African Student
Airlift, 1959

Arrival in the USA

With so much activity and the high level of African involvement, this single event – the departure of eighty one African students for the United States and Canada in a single chartered aircraft – was the media highlight of the year for Kenya. Due to the efforts by many to downplay or overtly oppose the departure, the hue and cry was intense. Colonial officials again complained about the 'lowering of standards' and unqualified students going to inferior schools overseas where they would receive a poor education that would be useless back in Kenya. The colonial government and the Education Department dragged their feet and placed obstacles in the way of students obtaining passports, though they abstained from blatant attempts to block their departure.

When the plane landed in New York, the Airlift again attracted extensive media coverage. It was featured by *Time* magazine and The *New York Times*. The students were interviewed at length. As the *Time* article clearly reflects, the press was fascinated by these young Africans from a distant and little-known culture: "Into the halls of USA higher education last week marched an exotic vanguard ... In Manhattan 81 students were busy answering reporters' questions ... In (a) clipped British accent, (a) Maasai tribesman reported that his hunting trophies included four cobras, two antelopes and a rhinoceros. But his tribal status, he explained, is still not high."

The attention from the press was a heady experience for the students, but they acquitted themselves well in their remarks. There was little time to bask in the spotlight however, they almost immediately dispersed to their schools, some of which were already in session.

There were some negative comments on that side of the Atlantic that reflected what had already been said in Kenya by the British. Dire predictions came from the elitists in the higher education councils in New York and Washington and in the international education organisations. These critics, most of whom had never been to Africa, spoke from a minimum of knowledge. Their views were coloured by having dealt only with the more advanced educational systems of Europe. More often than not they took their cues from the British.

The organisers of the Airlift were accused of political motivations for advancing certain African politicians, and of sending students to schools where they would surely fail. Those with direct knowledge of the students, however, knew that, except for the few going to high school who would stay with American families, all possessed the Cambridge School Certificate and were fully admissible to any school in the USA or Canada.

The more substantial issue was whether they could adjust to the American system of education. They had already succeeded in the demanding British curriculum that was often irrelevant to Kenyan needs, so their resiliency and adaptability had been tested. Nevertheless, the sudden transition would be both dislocating and intimidating. Could they adjust quickly enough to the less structured, self-directed curricula in America?

Certainly during the first year a number of the students struggled academically, culturally, socially, and often financially. The lack of formal orientation and the absence of any settling in period hampered their adjustment. But once they learnt a few of the ground rules in the American educational system, they bounced back and achieved outstanding results.

Of the original eighty one on the '59 airlift, sixty eight were men and a surprising thirteen were women. I was unable to trace two of the men, Abdulrasul Samma from Tanganyika and Yunus Mpagi from Uganda. Information was collected on seventy of the remaining seventy nine (89%). No data were available on the other nine, including three of the five men who went to Canada. Four of the seventy nine were bound for high schools in the USA. Three of these were women, reflecting the fact that women's education in Kenya had been sadly neglected, even more so than the men's.

Some went South

The eighty-one students scattered across the country from Maine to California and from Wisconsin to Texas. Their schools ranged from Bowdoin, Purdue, Howard, and the University of Chicago to others like Moravian College in Pennsylvania, Philander-Smith in Little Rock, Arkansas, Jarvis Christian College in Hawkins, Texas, and Diablo Valley Community College in California.

Thirteen went to schools in the 'Deep South', Tuskegee (3), Atlanta University (6) and Philander-Smith (4). This part of the programme gave rise to even more criticism. The fear was expressed by some in the international educational exchange circles that even if these students were not directly embroiled in the racial strife then occurring in places like Little Rock, they would inevitably suffer discrimination and perhaps other indignities, and they would return home (as predicted years before by Alliance High School headmaster Carey Francis), disillusioned with the United States.

What these 'experts' failed to take into account was that Kenya had its own version of apartheid: 'pass laws', and segregated housing, schools, hospitals, hotels and restaurants. Far greater discrimination and separation of the races existed in Kenya than in the United States, even in the deep South. As one student later said, "It wouldn't have bothered us. We were used to it!"

Some American educational leaders also greatly underestimated the resilience of these Africans and their ability to move about in the flexible American educational system in order to achieve their objectives. All of the students who went South (except for two students I was unable to contact) completed at least a bachelor's degree, although not always at the schools where they initially enrolled. Without exception, these students later returned to Kenya.

The Philander-Smith experience

The four students who headed to Philander-Smith College in Little Rock arrived at the small black Methodist school at a time of increased racial tension. None had any previous knowledge of Philander-Smith, nor were they aware that it was an all-black school, though when I interviewed them in 1988[15] they said this would not have mattered. When they arrived in the United States, a *New York Times* reporter had asked them, "Why Little Rock?"

One student, Frank Nabutete, offered a candid answer: "I want to experience what is there. Troubles are not in Little Rock alone ... The trouble in Little Rock might give me a better experience for when I return to Kenya ... When I told my friends I was going to Little Rock to study ... they all said I might fall in danger there. But there really is not much

---

15 I returned to Kenya for four months in 1987, after I retired and had the time to do the research and conduct the interviews for this book. I visited Kenya again for two months in 1996 for follow-up research. The delays since then were due to my intermittent health problems.

difference between Little Rock and Kenya. In schools in Kenya we do not have Africans learning together with Europeans. The African in Kenya could not go into a European hotel. The main trouble in Kenya is that the three races – the Whites, Asians and Africans – cannot work together."

The four were well received at Philander-Smith; only later did three of them begin to realise that they could not pursue their desired course of study at a small liberal arts college. Thus, they began to explore other possibilities. Only Daniel Maundu remained at the college to earn a degree. He later went to a seminary and returned to Kenya. He became a pastor of a church in Limuru on the outskirts of Nairobi.

Ellistone Mngola Kiwinda transferred to the University of Wisconsin to obtain his degree. When he came home to Kenya, he joined the Foreign Service and became the Ambassador to Zaire before he died in 1969.

Nabutete, the student who had made the statement in New York, also went to the University of Wisconsin, where he finished his first degree. Before returning to Kenya, he studied law in Britain. Back in Kenya he rose in the Attorney General's office to become Queens' Counsel[16]. In 1987 he went to Canada for an advanced degree in international law. He is now an advocate practising in Nairobi.

The most interesting story is that of Samuel Mutisya Ngola. In 1957, Ngola finished high school in Kenya with good grades. But, the only opportunity available was a three-year training course at Nairobi's King George VI Hospital (now Nairobi Hospital) to become a health inspector. Shortly after starting the course, he was accepted at the Royal Technical College (now University of Nairobi). However, he was not permitted to drop out of the health inspector course to enrol at the College. This angered him so much that he was determined to seek higher education outside the country.

However, there was a problem. According to Ngola, the police were routinely picking up school boys (distinguished by their universal uniform – shorts) and turning them away when they tried to enter the American Consulate building on Government Road (now Moi Avenue). In order for him not to be turned away, he dressed in long pants and made his way without interference to the Cultural Affairs Office, which at the time was in the Consulate building. As a result of that visit, he applied to several colleges and with the help of the District Commissioner of his home area and sponsorship by Tom Mboya, he enrolled with a scholarship at Philander-Smith.

---

16 Now feted as Senior Counsel.

At the end of his first year, in the summer of 1960, he took a bus tour of several Mid-Atlantic States,[17] during which he visited Marshall College in Huntington, West Virginia. He was impressed by the school, especially since it offered a Bachelor of Science in Business Administration, a degree not available at Philander-Smith. However, he was already committed to stay at Philander-Smith for the upcoming year, and so he returned to Little Rock. Through the school, he found work and lodging at the home of a leading Little Rock banker. In return for the maintenance work he did at the white banker's home, his second year was paid for.

The banker took a great liking to Ngola and helped him in numerous ways. He was distressed by the racial violence and discrimination against blacks in Little Rock, which were hurting business and giving Arkansas a bad name. Furthermore, he disapproved of the way Governor Orval Faubus of Arkansas (1955 to 1967) had handled the issue of school integration. In 1957 the Governor had stood at the entrance to Little Rock High School, barring admission to black students and forcing the federal government to send in troops.

The banker believed that something had to be done. He knew Governor Faubus well, so he arranged to have tea with him and took Ngola along. During this meeting, the banker took the Governor to task for his discriminatory policies. He pointed out that students like Ngola were, in effect, ambassadors from their own countries; it was disgraceful for them to witness racial discrimination or be treated in any discriminatory way in the United States. Governor Faubus appeared to listen to what the banker was saying, and Ngola believed that the visit had played a constructive role in improving the racial climate in Little Rock thereafter.

Toward the end of his second year, Ngola concluded that he needed to transfer to a school where he could major in business. Both the banker and Bishop Brown at Philander-Smith tried to persuade him to stay, but in the end they helped him switch to Marshall College and arranged for his financing. He received his degree in Business Administration in 1963 and was accepted at the University of New Mexico for a Master's degree in Industrial Administration, which he achieved in 1964. After further study in Economics at the University of Oregon, he returned to the University of New Mexico on a teaching assistantship and pursued a Doctorate in Economics.

---

17 The Mid-Atlantic States form a region of the United States generally located between New England and the South Atlantic States. The region often includes Delaware, Maryland, New Jersey, Pennsylvania, Washington D.C., New York, Virginia, West Virginia and sometimes North Carolina.

By this time he had married Gillian, a tall, red-haired, white American woman from Oregon. The first of their five children, all born in the United States, arrived in 1971. Faced with growing family responsibilities and limited resources, Ngola could not spend full time on a PhD. He divided his time between the teaching assistantship and teaching Kiswahili, and was eventually awarded a PhD in Economics in 1979.

Having acquired three degrees, a wife and five children, and having spent twenty years in the United States, Ngola was anxious to return home. He applied to the University of Nairobi, and in 1980 was accepted as a Lecturer in Economics. By 1987, he was a full professor.

Ngola was most laudatory about the United States and particularly about the educational system, which afforded a person with limited means, like himself, an opportunity to reach the highest level of academic achievement. He gratefully acknowledged the help he had received from the many friends he had made there.

Though all the students who went South were specifically asked, none reported discrimination against them or any involvement in racial incidents, except the Ngolas. Their only negative experiences had occurred during a year when they both taught at Tugaloo University in Mississippi. They lived in a cottage on campus, and so were protected from the worst of the racism in a small Mississippi town, but when they first went grocery shopping together they were subjected to unpleasant harassment.

"So we stopped doing that and I went alone," Gillian says. "But one day I had my baby daughter with me. An old woman stopped by the cart and said, 'How did your little girl get such a suntan this time of year?'

"She asked it innocently, but a *redneck* in the next aisle pricked up his ears and looked me and the baby over, then followed us through the store and out of the door. He jumped in his truck and followed closely behind my car to the edge of town. Then he gunned his engine, roared past me, and swung suddenly in front of me, trying to cut me off. I was terrified! I never again took the baby to town while I was there."[18]

Gillian said it was a dreadful year and she was very glad when it ended.

Others who went South

At Atlanta University and Tuskegee Institute, most of the students stayed to earn bachelor's degrees. The one exception was Nicholas Raballa. Prior to coming to the USA, Raballa was enrolled at Makerere

---

18 "Followed closely in back of my car" means his car was very close behind Gillian's. "Gunned the engine" means he pushed hard down on the accelerator.

College, which was still not awarding degrees. He therefore, sought a way to continue his education outside of East Africa. He was accepted with a scholarship at Tuskegee, the oldest black school in the South. He made many friends there, including Dr Martin Luther King, Jr, and was a guest in Dr King's home in Alabama. However, he felt that in view of his two years of college at Makerere, he needed a more demanding course of study than Tuskegee could provide. He transferred to Hope College, a small liberal arts Quaker school in Holland, Michigan. His original goal had been to major in Science, but since he lacked the requisite high school preparation and laboratory experience, he soon discovered how difficult that would be. Instead he graduated from Hope in 1965 with a Bachelor of Arts in History.

At the time, a manpower team from Kenya was touring the USA to recruit Kenyan students for government positions. Raballa was offered a District Officer's post in the Provincial Administration, but he was not interested in a job that would isolate him in a remote part of Kenya. Instead, he went to Canada and joined Osgoode Hall in Toronto for legal studies.

Financing was not easy. He spent three years working part-time and pursuing the course, only to find that the Kenyan government would not qualify him for the Kenyan Bar. Canadian law was not, at the time, compatible with Kenya law, which followed the British system. To qualify, Raballa had to finish his legal education at the Inns of Court in London. There, he completed two years of the three-year course, but he lacked the five hundred pounds sterling for the third year.

Fortunately, a friend from Canada visited him about that time and seeing his plight, generously provided the necessary fees and a monthly living allowance. Raballa finished his legal studies in 1972, returned to Kenya, and secured a position in the Attorney General's office. After serving there for five years, he went into private practice. Raballa's was yet another case of hard work, persistence, and the valuable assistance of new-found friends along the way.

Some became Californians

Due to Dr Kiano's efforts, seven of the eighty-one Airlift students wound up in the San Francisco Bay area. They included; Evanston Gichuhi, Elizabeth and George Kamau, Francis Githaiga, James Kungu, Gladwell Muthoni, and Beatrice Njuguna. Having been at the University of California Berkeley for a number of years, Kiano had made many friends. He was particularly close to his doctoral committee chairman, Dr Robert Scalapino and his wife Dee, both of whom had visited Kiano in Nairobi in 1958. They later agreed to sponsor seven students from the '59 Airlift. Mrs Scalapino found housing with local families where the students worked for room, board, and a little spending money. It was too late for admission to a state college, so except for Beatrice who was to attend high school, Mrs Scalapino arranged for them to be enrolled at Diablo Valley Community College in Walnut Creek, some forty kilometres from Berkeley.

Mrs Scalapino herself drove the eighty kilometre round trip twice a day to take the students back and forth to school. She became the group's 'Mother Superior', counsellor, financial agent, and psychologist. Each afternoon she found time to discuss with the students the day's problems and concerns. One Saturday morning after the students had been there for several months, she met with three of the men at their request 'to discuss various things'. The meeting took place at the Scalapinos' home and lasted five hours. The students asked all sorts of questions about things that puzzled them – social relations in the USA, dating, sex, customs, and handling money. Afterwards, they told Mrs Scalapino that they had never in their lives spoken about such subjects to a woman. In their African society, it was unheard of to discuss such issues openly.

Impressed with how well the students were doing, Mrs Scalapino set up the non-profit Committee for African Students to help them. It consisted of seventeen whites and seventeen blacks: ministers, doctors, social workers, professors, the head of the Oakland National Association for the Advancement of Coloured People (NAACP), a lawyer, the Dean of the Business School at the University of California, a Kaiser Medical Foundation surgeon who was instrumental in securing health insurance coverage, and a local Certified Public Accountant (CPA who contributed his services to maintain the Committee's tax exempt status.

Fund raising was begun to provide money for books, tuition, and other school related expenses. The task was not easy. Each semester Mrs Scalapino mailed out a fund raising letter, and both she and her husband, as well as some of the students, gave lectures at civic clubs and church gatherings. Each year barely enough money was raised to meet the expenses. California did not offer scholarships to international students, but through a friend who was the administrative assistant to Governor Pat Brown of California (1905–1996), the Scalapinos made an appeal to the Governor and The University of California's Board of

Regents. The result was a number of scholarships funded by personal contributions from members of the Board of Regents.

The number of students kept growing. By 1961, the Committee had assisted a total of forty eight Kenyans to go to the Bay area. At that point, members of the Committee committed themselves to seeing the forty eight through to graduation from a four-year college course. It was an impressive community effort and of great benefit to the students, who were assured of support until they graduated.

One other student in this group was Evanson Gichuhi. Like that of so many others, his path was not easy. He had graduated from Alliance High School in 1954, but although he had always been among the top ten in his class, he did not receive a grade high enough in English to be accepted at Makerere College.

He said when interviewed,

> "My English teacher at Alliance took a dislike to me. I never understood why. He consistently gave me failing grades, until one day I copied the paper of a top student and turned it in as my own. The other student got the top grade of 16. I received a failing grade of 6. When I confronted the teacher he turned very red, but he had nothing to say."

Gichuhi was outraged. A heavily built, outspoken man with a broad smile, he shook his head at the memory.

> "That year turned me against English composition for life," he remarked. "I've detested writing in English ever since."

He was determined to obtain a college education nevertheless, and gave himself ten years to accomplish it. At the time, the only other opportunity for further education was in teacher training colleges. Unlike similarly named American institutions, these were not really colleges and led only to a qualification to teach in an African primary or middle school. With no other option, Gichuhi completed the course at Kagumo Teachers Training College and stayed on for a short time to teach Science. Here too, he found a situation that irked him. "The European teachers at Kagumo had indoor bathrooms and flush toilets, but African teachers were supposed to use outhouses," he said.

> "What did they think we were?" he said indignantly. "We had had indoor plumbing at Alliance. We knew how to use flush toilets. What was this place out there that we were supposed to use?"

In Gichuhi's class at Kagumo, all but two succeeded in going overseas and getting degrees. Gichuhi was scheduled to enrol at Lincoln University in Pennsylvania in 1958 on a scholarship arranged through the university president, Dr Horace Mann Boad, with the help of Gichuhi's friend and a Lincoln alumnus, Kariuki Njiiri. Unfortunately, twenty four hours before his scheduled departure, his seat on the airplane 'disappeared'. It was too late to make other plans, and he was unable to go.

"Someone else took my place," he said. "I never knew who, but I think perhaps there was some nepotism there."

The following year, with Kiano's help, he left on the '59 Airlift, bound for California and Diablo Valley. He was so afraid of another disappointment that he told his parents and friends not to come to the airport to see him off.

"I didn't really believe I was going until the pilot announced that we had left the Kenyan airspace. I thought, even after we took off, that the plane might be called back."

As arranged by Dee Scalapino, Gichuhi lived with families in the East Bay area and later transferred to Contra Costa College and then to San Francisco State. His original goal was to study medicine, but like Nicholas Raballa and others, he learnt that he lacked the rigorous Science background required in the United States. In addition, given the cost required of medical school and the time, medicine was not a feasible career choice. Instead, he graduated in 1964 with a Bachelor of Science in Mathematics and Chemistry.

Meanwhile, Gichuhi had met and married another Kenyan student, Florence Chutha, who had come on the second Student Airlift in 1960. Their first child was born in 1962, and their financial situation was precarious. The Committee for African Students was committed to raising money for schooling, but had no resources to care for families. Gichuhi at the time had about USD$12 in his bank account. Concerned about the hospital bill, he went to the hospital administrator and got a job as a janitor in order to pay off his debt. During the summer he also worked in a tomato-canning factory. He said the experience was fascinating, right out of the Charlie Chaplin movie, *Modern Times*, which showed the mind-numbing and dehumanising effect of factory work on men operating impersonal assembly line machines.

After graduating in 1963, Gichuhi obtained a well paying job teaching Kiswahili at the Army Language School in Monterey. Shortly thereafter, however, he received a telegram from the Kenya Ministry of Education offering a three-year posting. He returned with his family in January 1965 to join the Ministry. His main responsibility was to keep track of Kenyan students going to the United States and the USSR to attend college. The position led to a two-year posting in the Kenyan Embassy in Moscow as an Educational Attaché. He found it to be an interesting but frustrating assignment. The Soviets often prevented him from contacting Kenyan students in Russia, or them from contacting him. This led to many students being subjected to ugly racial harassments. Some twenty years later, Gichuhi remarked that his tenure in Moscow, where he spent a little over a year, was so difficult and frustrating that it felt 'more like ten years'.

The students finally took matters into their own hands, went public with their complaints, and demanded to return home. According to Gichuhi, the Russian government stalled for a while, but eventually the students were put aboard Aeroflot planes and flown home. With the intervention of Gordon Hagberg of the Institute of International Education (IIE), who was also a former highly respected head of USIS in Nairobi, fifteen of the students from Russia were able to continue their education in the States.

After Moscow, Gichuhi was transferred to the same position in London. He returned home in 1970 to become the Assistant Registrar at the University of Nairobi. For the next six years, he occupied registry positions both there and at the newly established Kenyatta University College. In 1977, he was appointed Registrar of the University of Nairobi, where he remained until 1983.

When interviewed in 1996, Gichuhi pointed out that his first child, the one born in the United States, finished dental school at the University of California, San Francisco. His second child studied law at the University of Dar es Salaam, Tanzania, and the third went to Leeds University in England. As he said, the family had a wonderfully diverse educational experience. He could not have been more positive about his own education and experiences in the USA. According to him, the students on the '59 Airlift had gone to America as ignorant schoolboys and schoolgirls. They had returned home, after many character-building experiences, educated and responsible men and women. Despite the difficulty of working and attending school, doing so had taught him the value of an education, and in the process he learnt one of the greatest lessons: self-discipline. He and his fellow students also learnt how to think, inquire, and make informed decisions for themselves. This view was echoed time and again by every one of those I interviewed.

Perhaps Gichuhi's most telling and insightful remark about the American experience was this:

> "We came back a different breed. Had it not been for the Airlift and opportunities like it, this country would never have made it."

He enjoyed telling a little story about himself. After independence, most of Kenya's rising middle class continued the colonial practice of having several servants, including a *shamba* 'boy', or gardener. But on weekends, Gichuhi loved to work in the garden himself. Occasionally, people would come to the house and ask him, "Where is the *Bwana* (Master)?"

Gichuhi would tell them, "He is not here!" Continues he: "I let them think I am the *shamba* boy!"

Others went to Canada

The experiences of those who went to Canada were no different. Simon Gichuru was aided by a Catholic bishop in Nairobi in his effort to attend St Francis Xavier University in Antigonish, Nova Scotia. Gichuru told how he and several other overseas students were also helped by a priest in the Canadian school. When no work could be found in Nova Scotia in the summer of 1960, the priest took them, at his own expense, across Canada on the Canadian National Railways in search of jobs. He helped Gichuru obtain work in a pulp mill in British Columbia. Gichuru related how he learnt what hard physical labour was, using a pick and shovel and living in a work camp all summer. He was very proud that he had responded to the challenge and had learnt to respect hard manual labour. He saved enough money that summer for the entire second year's expenses. Thereafter, for the remainder of his education in Canada, he worked every summer in construction jobs.

For him, the Airlift was a revelation. It opened new horizons that he had not dreamed of as possible. As he said, "It was the turning point of my life." He married a Canadian girl and they had two children while in Canada. He returned to Kenya in 1968 to occupy a high post in the Ministry of Commerce and Industry, where he was in charge of international trade. Later, he was the Kenya Commercial Attaché in Washington DC for five years and travelled through thirty four states and Latin America. He mixed with people of all colours and gained a deep appreciation of the rights and freedoms that Americans enjoyed.

Gichuru remained in the Ministry of Commerce and Industry for the rest of his civil service career. He and his wife sent all their four children to universities in Canada to study medicine, economics, and science.

One of Gichuru's compatriots in Canada, who attended and graduated from McGill University, was John Mbugua. He later became the Kenyan Ambassador to the United States during the time when Gichuru also served in Washington DC.

So far as I could learn, all those who went to Canada experienced the same success as their counterparts who were in the United States.

Some staffed Kenya's diplomatic service

Five of the students on the '59 Airlift, including John Mbugua, Nicholas Mugo, Simon Kairo, Jennifer Ragwar, and Ellistone Mngola Kiwinda, returned to Kenya and subsequently entered Kenya's budding diplomatic service. Over the course of their careers, all the five became ambassadors.

Nicholas Mugo, helped like others by Dr Kiano, went to the USA to attend Warren Wilson College, a junior college in Swannanoa, North Carolina. His needs were covered by a work scholarship. He was on the Dean's list all the time he was there and finished with an Associate in Arts[19] degree in 1961. With his excellent record, he was awarded a full scholarship from the National Board of Presbyterian Missions to attend Lincoln University.

His wife Beth, as often happened to the wives of the Airlift students, was left at home in Kenya. Most of the women had not attended secondary school and hence their placement in the United States was more difficult to arrange. With the help of the Presbyterian Board, however, Beth Mugo was able to join her husband in Pennsylvania, where she finished high school and went on to graduate from a business college in Wilmington, Delaware.

With additional help from the publisher of the local newspaper, *The Kennett Square Advertiser*, Nicholas graduated with honours from Lincoln. When the Mugos returned to Kenya in 1963, Nicholas joined the Foreign Service.

In the nine years that followed, he held a number of posts, including Under Secretary in the Ministry of Foreign Affairs, Acting High Commissioner in London, and Kenya delegate to the United Nations

---

19 A student who completes a two-year program can earn an Associate of Arts (AA) or an Associate of Science (AS) degree.

(UN). In 1973, he was appointed Kenya's Ambassador to Ethiopia, to the Organisation of African Unity (OAU) based in Addis Ababa, and to the Sudan. Later he served as ambassador to France, United Nations Educational, Scientific and Cultural Organisation (UNESCO), Yugoslavia, and the Vatican.

At the request of President Jomo Kenyatta, Mugo left the Foreign Service in 1978 to become the first Kenyan General Manager of the Sugar Corporation in Kenya and later Managing Director of the Textile Industry of Kenya. He retired from public service in 1983 to go into private business. Both the Mugos have been successful in business. Beth Mugo helped organise the Business and Professional Women's Association of Kenya and later became its president. Two of their children were educated in the USA and one in Britain.

One more remarkable tale of hard work and persistence against the odds emerged from the Foreign Service group. Simon Thuo Kairo had finished high school in Uganda but failed to gain one of the limited places at Makerere. For two years he worked as a clerk in Nairobi. As he said, "What other kind of job could we (Africans) get back then?"

Kairo knew and admired Kariuki Njiiri, who had recently returned home from Lincoln University. With help from Njiiri, Dr Kiano, and myself as Cultural Affairs Officer, he was admitted to North East Missouri State College in Kirksville, a small former teachers' college, and left on the '59 Airlift. His response to colonial criticisms of the Airlift was, "What would they have us do? We had no opportunity to further our education in Kenya."

After a year at North East Missouri State, he found a job in New York City with the help of William Scheinman and enrolled at Long Island University. More assistance came from another friend, a Dr Collins, who helped Kairo bring his wife Nellie and their two children to the United States that summer.

While attending Long Island University, Kairo went to school and worked during the day, then baby-sat while Nellie attended classes at night. New York was expensive, however, and a difficult environment in which to raise a family. So again with the help of Dr Collins, "... who made sure we had something to live on," and that of some Presbyterian friends, Kairo transferred on a full scholarship to Huron College, a Presbyterian school in South Dakota. The Kairos were the only blacks in the small town of Huron and the first Africans the townspeople had ever

Robert F Stephens

Robert F Stephens, Tom Mboya and Dr Fred Burke, former Director of Eastern African Studies, Syracuse University

Robert F Stephens and Tom Mboya

Left to right: Hank Toluzzi of NBC, Tom Mboya, Dr Julius Kiano and George Wilson Nthenge

The Airlifters

Alfred Kimangano Lyaro

Alividza Mugone

Amram Onyundo

Angelina Wokabi

Apollo Wakianga

Apolonia Peresira

Arthur Magugu

Arthur Wagithuru Mungai

Arthur Ruenyi

Beatrice Wairimu

Benjamin Oduor

Boaz Harrizon Ogola

Boniface Odero Nyimli

Chanzu

Cyrus Karuga

Daniel Thairu

Dorcas Boit

Dunstan Ireri

Elisha Otieno Otono

Elizabeth Kamau

Ellistone K Mngola Kwinda

Fedha Nathan

Francis Lewis Githaiga

Francis Santiago

Frank H Nabutete

Fred Dalizu Egambili

Eliena Mshana

Fue Nisaghurwe

Geoffrey Mariaso Maloiy

George Gichigi Kamau.

George Mwutho Warui

George Philip Ochola

Gulam Onyundo

Gladwelll Gathonio

Harrison Bwire Muyin

Henry Chege Karanja

Isania Kimaindo

Jackson Otieno

James Kungu

James Stephen Mugweru

Jenniffer Ragwar

John Indagwa

John Joseph Ocheng

John Kang'ethe

John Mutua Ngumbi

Johanson Mbithi

Joram Harry Karobia

Joseph Bern Magucha

Margaret Karigaca

Mary Gichuru

Moses Tenga Ole Marima

Ng'ethe Sarah

Nicholas Muratha Mugo

Nicholas Raballa

Ochieng Menya

Otieno Olero

Pamela Odede Mboya

Patricia Ododa

Paul Muthee

Peter Wachira

Philip Kihimba Maundu

Philip Ochieng

Raheir Wallace Murungi

Raphael Fredrick Omondi

Regina Katungulu

Rose Gichoki

Rueben Olembo

Sam Ramtu

Gitatha Samuel

Samuel Mutisya Ngola

Satischandra panachand Shah

Shadrack Ojudo Kwasa

Simon Kairo

Simon Mbai

Solomon Masembwa

Wilson Ndolo Ayah

Gordon Hagberg, Political Affairs Officer at USIS, Nairobi circa 1956/1957, Mower, Educational and Cultural Affairs Officer, USIS and an unidentified person.

Gordon Hagberg, two unknown people, Dr Kiano and Earnestine Kiano, and Jack Mower, 1956/1957 at USIS, Nairobi.

Jomo Kenyatta at a rally after his release from prison. Dr Kiano is in glasses.

Tom Mboya at a political rally, taken in 1958/1959

seen. They took the family under their wing, bringing them food and warm clothing for the cold Dakota winter, baby-sitting with the children, and giving them free tuition at the nursery school for the two years they were there. The Kairos were invited into local homes and formed friendships that, when I interviewed them in 1988, had lasted more than twenty five years.

"We heard about discrimination in the States," Nellie says, "but we were treated well."

Kairo graduated with a BA in Political Science in February, 1963. He returned home immediately, without the family, and was posted to Beijing, China, to open Kenya's embassy there. Nellie stayed in the United States to get her teaching certificate, then she and the family joined Kairo in China. He was appointed a year or so later as ambassador to the Organisation of African Unity (OAU) in Addis Ababa. Following this, he left the diplomatic service to go to the East African Common Services Organisation (EACSO), but was soon offered the post of private secretary to President Jomo Kenyatta. In 1974, he successfully contested elections for Parliament and won. He remained a Member of Parliament for five years.

In 1979, with his five children now approaching the costly university years, Kairo went into private business. Income from the businesses and the farms he had acquired gave the family a degree of comfort that a civil servant's salary could not approach. The Kairos' two eldest children went to Syracuse and St Lawrence Universities in New York State. Nellie worked as a teacher and later became an educational supervisor in Kiambu. In 1987, drawing on her experience in the United States, she established Kenya's first rural nursery school in Kiambu, outside of Nairobi. Her intent was that it becomes a model for the development of other rural schools.

Kairo, like so many others, had only positive things to say about his experiences in the United States. Also like so many others, he prided himself in having learnt how to work hard. He credited his time in the United States for shaping his life and carrying him forward to success back in Kenya.

As mentioned previously, Ellistone Mngola Kiwinda served as Ambassador to Zaire and John Mbugua as ambassador to Washington DC. Jennifer Ragwar was posted to Paris as Kenya's representative to UNESCO.

Others went into private business and industry

Working in government was not the only career to which the Airlifters aspired. Several students majored in business administration or economics, and during the Africanisation of private industry, a significant number were recruited. Even those who accepted government positions often later went into private industry or began business ventures of their own.

One of the latter was Adonijah Ochieng Menya. After graduating from Alliance High School in 1951 and lacking one point for admission to Makerere, he became, first, a railroad stationmaster and then a bookkeeper for the Kenya Farmers Association (KFA) – (an all-white settler organisation) in Nakuru, one hundred and sixty one kilometres Northwest of Nairobi and the centre of commerce in the Rift Valley. He had learnt bookkeeping by correspondence, but now wanted further education and began applying to American colleges. He was admitted with a tuition scholarship to San Francisco State College but needed transport, which the Airlift provided, and a place to live. Again through the efforts of Dr Kiano, Menya lived with a lawyer and his family in Presidio Heights. For four years, he worked in the family's home for his room and board. In the summers, he also worked as a bookkeeper at a local branch of the Bank of America to pay his school fees and other living expenses. At the time of his graduation, the Kenya recruitment team came to California and interviewed him. Impressed with his academic record, they recommended that he goes for a Master's degree on an Agency for International Development (AID) scholarship. He finished his Master's degree in Public Administration in nine months and won an award for the best Master's thesis that year at the University of Southern California.

In 1964 Menya returned home to become a District Officer in the Provincial Administration. He soon had many other job offers and chose to accept a position as Planning Officer at the University of East Africa (Makerere). Later, he spent two years as Chief Financial Officer of the Kenya National Trading Corporation (KNTC), and then moved on to be Managing Director of the Cotton Lint and Seed Marketing Board (CLSMB). In 1974 he set up his own business, a highly successful commodity trading firm, and became Chairman and Managing Director of Menya Associates, Ltd.

Menya had married an American woman while in school and was proud of the fact that his first three children had been educated in the United States.

The women went too

Unfortunately, women's education had a very low priority in Kenya. Few schools for girls existed, but even more important, these schools were not free. Any available money in a family usually went to pay the school fees for the chosen son or sons. The role of women in the African society of the 1950s was limited to bearing children, working on the *shambas* (farms), harvesting crops, gathering wood, and drawing water from sources that were frequently kilometres from their homes. Girls were expected to assist their mothers until they married.

A few girls succeeded in attending mission schools, but their education rarely extended beyond Standard (Grade) Six. It took great determination to continue beyond that point. Additionally, a high school for African girls was very late in coming – not until 1952, some twenty-five years after the founding of Alliance High School for boys. If a family was fairly well off, a girl would be sent to a private, usually mission, school in India or Uganda, but in the 1950s this was rare. In fact, there was not one African woman with a degree in all of Kenya at that time.

The inclusion of thirteen women in the '59 Airlift was, therefore, a significant step forward. It came about partly because the few educated men, some of whom were rising African politicians, came to realise that most women of marriageable age were uneducated, even to high school level.

Such a gap would make it difficult for the wife to be a true partner, capable of coping successfully in the fast-changing scene evolving in Kenya.

Three women on the Airlift (Mary Gichuru, Kathleen Mwihia, and Beatrice Njuguna) went directly to live with American families and attend high schools. Others had to play catch-up in some subjects before they could be admitted to a regular college degree programme, even though, some of them had the rough equivalent of a high school diploma. Wives of several Airlifters, like Beth Mugo, went later and attended high schools where their husbands were enrolled in college.

One of the three on the Airlift who went to high school was Mary Gichuru, the daughter of James Gichuru, a teacher and one of the early political leaders of Kenya. At Independence he became Kenya's first Minister for Finance. Mary was studying in India, but her father wanted her to have an opportunity to study in the United States. Arrangements were made for her to live with a couple in Newtonville, Massachusetts, where she attended Newton High School. She adapted well, and within one year had her diploma. She was accepted at Boston University with a scholarship from the African-American Institute. A year later, she won a full scholarship at Macalester College in St Paul, Minnesota and completed a BA degree in Sociology in 1964.

She returned to Kenya and was offered a position as a Community Development Officer in the Ministry of Social Services. Later she was made head of the Kenya Conference Centre (now Kenyatta International Convention Centre (KICC)), where the World Conference on the UN Decade for Women was held in 1985. As a result of her work, she was appointed to the Public Service Commission of Kenya. Women were, at last, beginning to receive deserved recognition in post-independence Kenya.

Kathleen Mwihia, whose story is told in Chapter Six, attended high school in Bethlehem, Pennsylvania, while her husband was enrolled at Moravian College. Beatrice Njuguna went to McKinley High School in Berkeley, California.

Another woman on the Airlift was Dorcas Boit. Dorcas had graduated from African Girls High School and from Siriba Teachers Training College before becoming a teacher. When she applied and was accepted at Spelman College in Atlanta, she was assigned a seat on the Airlift. After graduating, she returned to Kenya and later became Deputy Director of the Kenya National Council of Social Services founded in 1964.

One of the outstanding women on the Airlift was Pamela Odede. Pamela was the daughter of Fanuel Walter Odede, a teacher and prominent early African leader. Because of his position and her superior school record, Pamela had been able to attend the African Girls High School. Her intelligence and excellent record there ensured her admission to Makerere University College in Uganda, one of the few Kenyan girls to attend. After two years, she had gained a level of poise, confidence, sophistication, and knowledge well beyond most African women in Kenya at that time. She was a natural for a scholarship to the United States. She came from the same area near Lake Victoria as Tom Mboya. Through Tom's political connection with her father, they had become friends. Tom helped her get a scholarship to Western College for Women in Oxford, Ohio, which was then the women's adjunct to Miami University.

Pamela spent two years there and received a BA degree in Sociology. She loved the college and her roommates – a Japanese, a Hawaiian, and a Sudanese who became her best friend and was destined to marry the man who later became the Prime Minister for the Sudan.

After graduation in 1961, Pamela returned to Kenya. She and Tom Mboya were married and began to raise a family. But then tragedy struck. On a Saturday afternoon in July of 1969, Tom walked out of a local pharmacy and was fatally shot, thus ending the life of one of Kenya's ablest leaders. Though a young Kikuyu man, Isaac Njenga Njoroge, was tried and executed for his murder, rumours continued to circulate that it was a political assassination and that others were involved. Nothing was ever proven and his death remains a mystery to this date.

Pamela was later appointed Kenya's Permanent Representative to Habitat, a UN agency headquartered in Nairobi, at the rank of Ambassador. In one of my interviews with her in 1988, she commented on the enormous value of the American education she and the other graduates had received.

> "Without the knowledge and training provided by the American graduates," she said, "Kenya could not possibly have developed as it has."

Pamela Mboya was working on her memoir when she died in January, 2009. Considering the place of African women in the Kenyan society prior to 1959, the total of nineteen women who went to America that year (thirteen on the Airlift and six privately) constituted nothing less than a revolution. These were the first African women in Kenya to obtain university degrees. Their impact on social organisation, education, economic activity, family structure and child-rearing in a changing culture was truly amazing. Their contributions were indispensable to the development of modern Kenya.

Chapter 6

Some special stories of the '59 Airlift

A married couple

On board the '59 Airlift was just one married couple, Francis and Kathleen Mwihia. The Mwihias were the only ones to come on immigrant rather than student visas. Because Kathleen was not yet enrolled in any college, she could not get a student visa. However, she knew she would have to work to help support herself and her husband, and for this she needed a green card,[20] obtainable only with immigrant or permanent resident status. She and Francis therefore applied for and received their immigrant visas.

In 1958, Francis had been attending Nairobi's Royal Technical College (now University of Nairobi), but he was determined to continue his education in the USA. At the USIS library he went through the American College and University Directory, writing down every school that gave scholarships to foreign students. He applied to several and was accepted at Moravian College in Bethlehem, Pennsylvania, with a tuition scholarship. However, he was unable to raise the money for transport and was forced to wait another year. Moravian then offered him a larger scholarship, and with this in hand he was able to claim a place for himself and his wife on the Airlift.

In Bethlehem, Kathleen not only worked but also attended high school part-time. There were many other married couples at Moravian and most wives, while also raising families, worked to help support their husbands. When Francis graduated two years later, Kathleen and the other wives received special framed diplomas, in recognition of the help and support they provided to their husbands.[21]

"After all," said Kathleen, "we had earned the degree too."

---

20 A United States Permanent Resident Card.
21 The wives received special diplomas in recognition of the help and support they provided to their husbands.

For Francis and Kathleen the achievement meant considerable personal sacrifice. To fulfil their dream of higher education, they had had to leave their first-born child behind with Francis' mother. This caused both of them great and continuing heartache.

Determined to pursue further studies, the Mwihias went to Chicago, where Francis worked for a labour union while he saved and tried to find support for graduate school. When he won the United States Agency for International Development (USAID) award, he enrolled at the University of Pittsburgh for a PhD in Economics and was subsequently selected for a prestigious Rockefeller Fellowship award. Meanwhile, Kathleen had finished high school in Chicago and continued her education at a college in Pittsburgh, where she took business administration.

Francis passed his comprehensive and oral exams and wrote part of his dissertation, but at this point he and Kathleen decided that it was time to go home. They had been away from their daughter and their families in Kenya for seven years, and in spite of their immigrant status, they had never intended to live permanently in the United States. Back in Kenya, Francis found a position with the Ministry of Finance and in time became its Academic Planning Director. Sometime after his return home he was notified by the University of Pittsburgh that some revisions of his dissertation were necessary. By this time he was immersed in his job and family and was regretfully unable to go back to the United States to finish the degree.

When her daughter and the son who had been born in the United States were old enough to go to school, Kathleen went to work as an administrator at the University of Nairobi. Both Francis and Kathleen later left government and worked together in a printing company they owned.

A brother and a sister

On the Airlift with the Mwihias were a brother and sister, George and Elizabeth Kamau. George and Francis Mwihia had been friends since they were students of Dr Kiano at the Royal Technical College (now University of Nairobi), and Kiano assisted them both to go to the States.

George and Elizabeth were part of the group that went to the San Francisco Bay area under the aegis of the Scalapinos. Elizabeth finished high school and college with a degree in Education. George did not stay long at Diablo Valley, but transferred to the University of California at Berkeley to major in Economics. He lived with Professor and Mrs

Hyde of the University of California and later with the Dupree family in Oakland, but he was determined to work and support himself. He found a job and worked seventeen hours a week but had to cut back when his grades began to suffer.

In the meantime, George had met Josephine Kanotha, a fellow Kenyan who came on the 1960 Airlift. Josephine had finished high school and was enrolled at a college in Oregon when she and George met. They were married just before George graduated from University of California, Berkeley in 1962. George, like Evanson Gichuhi, found a job teaching Kiswahili at the Army Language School in Monterey. Josephine transferred to San Jose State and graduated with a BA degree in Sociology in 1965.

Lisa, their first child was born in 1963, and though they were having a hard time making ends meet, George went on to pursue a master's degree. At the same time, he worked in the accounts division of the General Motors plant in Fremont, California. Finances were still tight, and much as he wanted to continue his graduate work, he knew that the job market for educated Kenyans was burgeoning back home. His close friend, Joe Wanjui, whose story was told in Chapter 3, was then Director of the Industrial and Commercial Development Corporation (ICDC). Founded by Dr Kiano, the ICDC was an offshoot of the Ministry of Commerce and Industry, of which Kiano was Minister, and was responsible not only for attracting new business and capital to Kenya but for building an entirely new industrial network.

Wanjui persuaded George to join the ICDC, where he soon became head of Loans and Investments. The mining side of the industry was developing quickly, so George moved over in 1972 to head the Continental Ore Kenya Limited where he set up a complete business from scratch. Another of his numerous projects was establishing a grain milling company. He resigned in 1980 and, with assistance from the World Bank; he formed a new industrial company to build a factory for the production of paper out of cotton, a cash crop in Kenya. In 1975, he became the Chief Executive of the Kenya National Chamber of Commerce and Industry (KNCCI).

Meanwhile, Josephine was employed in the Registrar's Office at the University of Nairobi. She and her former college roommate, Priscilla Njeri, (wife of former Ambassador to Ethiopia, Peter Icharia, also American-educated) talked to me at some length in 1988 about their experiences in the States. Both women described the shock of being plunged into Western culture and an American college.

"We were just village girls; we knew nothing," said Josephine. "But the Americans were wonderful to us. The family I lived with took such an interest in me. They did not look down on us at all, but just appreciated us for what we were."

She went on to say, "I am very indebted to the people of the United States for my education and all that they did for me. Anything I can do to pay back the many kind people, I will be more than happy to do. It is my great obligation. Every year since we came back we have had an American exchange student living with us. It's the least we can do."

Josephine and Priscilla both said that they had gone to America to learn to become better teachers, but when they enrolled at Oregon State University, they were frightened that they would not be able to do the work. After the first few months they realised that it was not so difficult and they could do it after all. Initially, they attended Mt Angel High School in Mt Angel, Oregon. They both graduated from San Jose State University in California with a Bachelor of Arts degree in 1965.

Priscilla said, "From then on we just did each thing as it came along. We learnt to meet challenges and win!"

As a result of their experiences in the United States, where they described the position of women as light years ahead of that in Kenya, these women and countless others who had similar experiences became committed feminists determined to be in the forefront of a new Kenya.[22] They were devoted to their families but unwilling to take a back seat as they had been forced to do before.

Josephine felt that the women of Kenya shared the same problems as other women all over the world: sex discrimination; difficulty in juggling jobs, marriage, and child rearing and lack of recognition of their abilities and contributions. But in Kenya, women had only recently awakened and realised how long their efforts had been unappreciated by men, and how much of the hard work of the country was actually being done by women. Josephine and Priscilla believed that if women educated their children – boys and girls alike – to share chores and responsibilities and have respect for each other; the women's lot would be much improved in the next generation. When her children were young, Josephine did away with the general practice of having servants. She did not want her children to grow up being waited on, not knowing how to take care of themselves. All four of her children learnt to cook, make beds, do laundry, clean the house and wash dishes.

---

22 The passage on the 2010 constitution has now given Kenyan women many opportunities.

In 1978, Josephine became a senior administrator in the Office of the Dean of Students at the University of Nairobi, and in 1985 she helped organise the UN Decade of Women Conference when she was secretary of the Kenya Association of Women. In 1988 she was selected as an exchange student at Penn State University for a Master's degree in Student Counselling.

Three of the Kamau's children have been educated in the United States. Lisa, the eldest, graduated from the University of California Berkeley in 1987 as a clinical dietician.

It would be difficult to find more worthwhile examples of the value of higher education than the Mwihias and the Kamaus.

A former Mau Mau suspect

One story that captured the media's attention in New York in 1959 was that of Cyrus Karuga. Karuga had been at Alliance High School from 1947 to 1951, and in 1952 he joined the Kenya African Union (KAU). Active in African politics, he became the assistant secretary for KAU. In this capacity he met Ira Morris, an American journalist and author visiting Kenya. A successful novelist living in France at the time, Morris was intrigued by this well-spoken African activist. After Morris left Kenya the two corresponded and a friendship developed.

This was at a time when the British had become convinced that KAU, with Jomo Kenyatta as its leader, was fomenting the Mau Mau rebellion that had just broken out. With the declaration of a State of Emergency in 1953, all the KAU leaders were seized and placed in detention as Mau Mau suspects. Karuga remained in detention for five years without trial, until 1958, when he was released. During his incarceration, which he believed was totally unjustified; he became determined to obtain a higher education. He had kept in touch with Ira Morris as best as he could and Morris, still in France, offered his support and Karuga was admitted to an American college. With help from Tom Mboya and Morris, Karuga was awarded a scholarship to Iowa Wesleyan and was given a place on the '59 Airlift. The story of his detention as a Mau Mau suspect had preceded him to New York, so by the time he arrived, he had already attained some degree of fame. He was interviewed by the press and appeared on both American Broadcasting Company (ABC) and National Broadcasting Company (NBC) during his week in New York before travelling on to Iowa Wesleyan.

After a year he transferred, with Morris's help, to Rutgers University where he graduated with a BA degree in Economics in 1963. He returned to Kenya in 1964 and when passing through London met Dr Kiano, then Minister for Commerce and Industry, who had just established the aforementioned Industrial and Commercial Development Corporation (ICDC). Kiano offered Karuga a position at ICDC, and for the next two years Karuga, like George Kamau, worked there before moving to the Ministry of Lands and Settlements. He later left government to set up his own business in the highlands North of Nairobi. In the newly independent Kenya, he was able to change any perception of himself as a Mau Mau rebel to that of an accomplished farmer and vigorous supporter of a free market economy.

A medical doctor

As many Americans can attest, a medical education is possibly the most difficult course to pursue in the United States. Medical schools are limited in number, admission standards are rigorous, and the course itself is lengthy, intense, and very costly. Not many foreign students could qualify for or afford medical school, and most Kenyan students in the 1950s in particular lacked the funds and the necessary Science background. One Airlifter who did achieve a medical degree was Samuel Abuna Ochola. He was admitted with a scholarship to the State University of New York (SUNY) at New Paltz. The first African student at New Paltz, he was on the Dean's List throughout his college career, graduating with a Bachelor of Science degree in 1963. With financial assistance from the African-American Institute, he went on to the Howard University Medical School in Washington, DC and was awarded his MD in 1967.

After an internship, he completed a surgical residency at Wayne State University-Grace Hospital in Detroit in 1972 and returned home to be a lecturer at the newly opened University of Nairobi Medical School. He later went into private practice and operated a clinic in Nairobi. Although Ochola was the only one of the '59 Airlift to become a doctor, many other Kenyans subsequently succeeded in doing so, including two of his own children. Both attended the University of Rochester, one in medicine and another in dentistry.

A special success story

A special success story of the '59 Airlift is that of Reuben James Olembo. Olembo came from Kakamega, a region close to Lake Victoria. Educated in mission schools, he finished secondary school with good grades and was admitted to the Royal Technical College in Nairobi, where he was president of the Student Council. He was also one of the few who attained a Cambridge Overseas School Certificate Division 1in 1956 and in 1959 took the London Advanced Level Examination, which qualified him for acceptance at a British university. He was promised a full bursary at St Andrews University in Scotland, but he was more interested in going to the United States. He feared that if he earned a degree in the United Kingdom he would be obligated to return home and be slotted into some secondary teaching position for the rest of his career.

He consulted Dr Kiano, who sent him to me at USIS. I provided him with a list of colleges to contact, along with a letter of recommendation and an evaluation of his academic credentials. The result was an acceptance from Purdue University for a degree in Natural Science. When word reached Peter Gale, the English Principal of the Royal Technical College (now University of Nairobi), Olembo was called into Gale's office and given a dressing down for refusing an opportunity to attend St Andrews University in favour of what Gale called an education of 'doubtful quality' at a school 'unknown and unrecognised in Kenya'. Olembo was also told by a high ranking official in the Kenya Education Department that he 'risked being recruited' in the USA and 'might be suspected of being a subversive on his return'.

Meanwhile the missionaries in his home area, and even his father, tried to persuade him to go to a church-related college in the United States. Olembo won them all over when it turned out that the foreign student advisor at Purdue, with whom Olembo had been corresponding, was a member of their same church. With tuition and fees granted by Purdue; room, board and incidentals by an Indianapolis foundation; some help from the African-American Institute; and a seat on the Airlift, Olembo took off for America. By 1961 he had his Bachelor of Science in Biology and Chemistry, and was admitted to graduate school. Like Maina Wanjigi and Francis Mwihia, he was granted a much-prized Rockefeller Foundation Fellowship. Just four years later, in 1965, he was awarded a PhD in Genetics with minors in Biochemistry and Statistics. It was an impressive achievement for anyone, but even more so for a Kenyan with little Science background, no laboratory experience, and almost no exposure to the advanced technological world.

He returned home with his PhD to a position as Lecturer in Botany at Makerere University, where he was given full responsibility for establishing courses in genetics for all university students in science, education, agriculture, and medicine. He switched to the University of Nairobi in 1970 and shortly became a full professor and chairman of the Botany Department.

In 1978 Olembo was combining his lecturing job with service in the United Nations Environment Programme (UNEP), headquartered in Nairobi. He moved permanently to UNEP in 1979 and was much in demand as a speaker. He also wrote extensively, served on many boards and international committees, and travelled the world. His case, as much as any, represents what can be accomplished by young men and women from an educationally impoverished society when given the opportunity to reach their full potential.

Nationhood, Africanisation and the effects of the 1959 Airlift

Many others on this Airlift, besides those already mentioned, returned soon after Kenya's independence in December, 1963, just as government, commerce and industry, agriculture, education, and other sectors were being Africanised. Manpower demands quickly outstripped the number of educated Africans available. Only a few years previously, no one had expected independence to come so quickly, not even African leaders like Tom Mboya and Dr Kiano. The colonial government had fully expected that the expatriate civil service would stay in place for many years, essentially running things under titular African ministers.

However, the new leadership was bent on Africanising as rapidly as possible and this meant that university-educated Africans were the objects of vigorous recruitment. In addition, with Independence came the expansion of government departments and agencies. New ministries came into being overnight: Foreign Affairs, Commerce and Industry, Economic Planning, Constitutional Affairs, Lands and Settlements, and so on. Starting a diplomatic service from the top down was no easy task, nor was it any easier for the other ministries.

Accordingly, the recruitment teams mentioned earlier, financed largely by the United States Agency for International Development (USAID), fanned out in several directions. Because the largest concentration of Kenyan students was in the USA and Canada, greater effort was centred there. There was an obvious benefit to those who had been in the USA and Canada prior to 1960. Since they were about to acquire their degrees and were natural candidates for high level positions, they would be on the inside track for promotion during the Africanisation that occurred from

1962 to1965. In essence, all of those who left Kenya in 1959 or before had the best opportunity to acquit themselves in substantial roles.

They made every use of those opportunities: over 80% of them played leading roles within the government and helped form the backbone of the new civil service. Said Ambenge Chanzu attained the position of Undersecretary in the Office of the President, Jackton Isige was the Ministry of Commerce, Trade Attaché in London, Silvano Onyango Ogessa became Managing Director of Kenya National Trading Corporation (KNTC), Nathan Washika Fedha was Chief Archivist and Harris Mule Mutio, one of the official USA Government grantees, served as Permanent Secretary in the Ministry of Finance.

Benefits to higher education

Institutions of higher learning in Kenya reaped the benefits of the Airlift. It is astounding to realise that twelve of those who arrived in the US in 1959, or 16%, achieved doctorates. They included Samuel Ngola who, as previously noted, became a professor of Economics at the University of Nairobi, and Geoffrey Ole Maloiy, one of the first two Maasais to go to the United States and the first to obtain a doctorate in Veterinary Science. Maloiy went on to pursue an illustrious career as a professor at the University of Nairobi, Dean of the Faculty of Veterinary Medicine, Chairman of the Department of Animal Physiology, and the author of many books and articles.

Many others were quickly recruited by the University of Nairobi, which was rapidly expanding after independence. Fred Dalizu had attended Lincoln University, and then transferred to Howard University where he majored in Political Science. While there, he married Jean, an African American, and after they returned to Kenya, he joined the faculty at the University of Nairobi in 1974 as a Lecturer in government.[23] Jean later worked at the American Embassy in Nairobi, and died in the bomb attack there in 1998.

Others who joined the faculty at the University of Nairobi were Daniel Thairu, professor of Agriculture; Shadrack Kwasa, who also served as Minister for Foreign Affairs; James Olembo, profiled earlier, who chaired the Chemistry Department, and Boaz Ogalla, who became a lecturer at the University.

---

23 He joined the University of Nairobi in 1974 as a Lecturer in Government.

In fact, higher education grew so fast that within two years, by 1965, an entirely new institution came into being. Kenyatta College, later became a full-fledged university in 1985. Robert Murungi became Vice Chancellor, and Venentio Kabachia, professor of Physical Chemistry, established the Department of Chemistry.

Two of those who arrived privately were also among those who earned doctorates. Eliud Maluki received his degree at the University of Denver, and Boaz Namasaka, whose story is told in the following chapter, was awarded a PhD by Claremont College.

The '59 group was merely the initial phalanx of American and Canadian graduates who were to staff all levels of and transform higher education in Kenya, as well as reform Kenya's entire educational system.

In my analysis of the '59 Airlift, as far as I learnt, only two of the eighty one failed and had to return home. Most important to note is that once the students graduated, a great majority of them returned to Kenya. Unfortunately, at the time of the interviews (1987-88 and 1996) twelve of the returnees to Kenya had died. Of those whom I could trace, sixty-three took up positions in Kenya just before or after self-government was granted on 1 June 1963. Only seven (9%) remained in the United States. Most of them had advanced degrees in specialties that could not then be utilised in Kenya.

It is an exceptional record for a programme that was condemned by the colonial government and forecast for failure by some in the American educational hierarchy. The influence these graduates had was integral to the development of their country.

Chapter 7

Others went too

In addition to the eighty one students on the '59 Airlift, eleven others received official USA Government scholarships that generally included travel, and another thirty four arranged their own scholarships and travel for a total of one hundred and twenty six students who went that year. It should be noted that one of those who travelled privately was Barack Obama Senior, father of the 44th President of the USA, Barack Obama. I interviewed Obama Senior briefly, but since he had not finished high school and lacked the required Cambridge School Certificate, he was not selected for an official scholarship nor for a seat on the 1959 Airlift. With the help of an American friend, Elizabeth Mooney, he made his own arrangements for a scholarship and travel to the University of Hawaii. There he met and married a fellow student, Ann Dunham. Barack Obama Junior was born six months later. He was a year old when his father left the family in Hawaii and entered a PhD programme at Harvard. Father and son saw each other only once more, when Barack Obama Junior was ten and his father went to Hawaii to visit. Barack Obama Senior later returned to Kenya, where he served as an economist in the government. He died in an motor accident in Nairobi in 1982.

On USA Government scholarships

For the first time, one of the USA Government scholarships went to a woman. Margaret Kabiru graduated from Western College for Women in Ohio and married Dr Peter Kamau soon after returning to Kenya. She began raising a family, ran a successful catering business for many years, and became Chairperson of the Business and Professional Women's Association of Kenya.

Another official grantee, Kyale Mwendwa, had been a schoolteacher before applying for the scholarship. He was accepted at Michigan State University, earned a master's degree, and went back to Kenya to work in the Ministry of Education. Later he was elected to Parliament and became Minister for Education.

Wilson Ndolo Ayah already had the equivalent of a BA degree when he was selected and had been working as a researcher for Marco Surveys Limited, a private polling and research organisation. He went to the University of Wisconsin, where he received a Master's degree in Agricultural Economics in 1962 and immediately returned home. In 1969 he too won a seat in Parliament. He was appointed Assistant Minister for Finance in 1987, and was later picked to be Minister for Research, Science and Technology in the same year. He was appointed to the water docket in 1988. He later took over the important post of Minister for Foreign Affairs and International Cooperation after the brutal murder of Dr Robert John Ouko in 1990.

A dream come true

Filemone Indire, another recipient of a USA Government scholarship, was one of those who later served in the Ministries of Education and Foreign Affairs. He was a highly regarded teacher at the American Quaker Mission School in Kaimosi, where he had taught (high school) for three years. The Mission School was four hundred and two kilometres from Nairobi and one hundred and twenty-nine kilometres North of Lake Victoria, tucked away in a rural area well off the beaten track. It had been established by the American Friends in 1902 – long before any other American religious connection had been made.

Early in 1959 Fred Reeves, the head of the Friends Mission, visited the Cultural Affairs Office in Nairobi. He was seeking assistance for Indire, whom he described as a bright young man who already had a Diploma in Education from Makerere University College and who would benefit greatly from graduate work at an American university.

By this time, the State Department's requirements had been modified sufficiently to allow someone with Indire's academic background and teaching experience to apply for an official USA Government scholarship. When I interviewed him, I found him articulate and intelligent. I highly recommended him for study. He was chosen from among a competitive group of applicants. Indire recalls that when Fred Reeves went to his family's home with the news, "We could hardly believe it. It was a dream come true!"

With a full Fulbright/Smith-Mundt grant, Indire first went to Ball State College in Indiana for an MA degree, then to Indiana University where in 1962, he received a PhD in Education. The Quakers had provided the financing for his wife Abigail and their three children to join him in Indiana, where Abigail was also able to attend college.

Indire's first job back in Kenya in 1962 was to oversee the establishment of a secondary school, modelled on an American high school, that was being built in his home area with USAID funds. Soon after, he was chosen by the Ministry of Education to be in charge of higher education and overseas scholarships. This was just the beginning of a varied and wide-ranging career. In 1964, he was seconded to the Ministry of Foreign Affairs. Because the newly independent government was concerned about the numbers of Kenyan students going to the Soviet Union and other Communist bloc countries, he was sent to Kenya's recently opened Embassy in Moscow and put in charge of Kenyan Student Affairs.

He soon encountered the same kind of problems in the Soviet Union that were faced by Evanson Gichuhi a little later. The students were isolated in remote or inferior institutions, subjected to racism, prevented from communicating with Indire or he with them, and complained of being indoctrinated with heavy doses of Marxism-Leninism.

The flood of Kenyan students to Communist countries had been a result of political controversies inside Kenya between Tom Mboya, Dr Kiano and others on the one hand and Communist-leaning Oginga Odinga on the other. A Luo, Odinga had been appointed Vice President by President Kenyatta, but he turned out to be something of a loose cannon. He began travelling outside the country and developing contacts with Soviet bloc countries, from whom he obtained a number of scholarships for Kenyan students. While such offers did not have the appeal of scholarships to America or Europe, to young Kenyans the chance to obtain further education was the ultimate determining factor, and many seized the opportunity.

Odinga meanwhile became embroiled in a bizarre incident at Nairobi's Embakasi Airport. The incident involved fifty scholarships for Kenyan students that had been offered, apparently through contact with Odinga, by the government of Bulgaria. The recipients were officially selected by the Ministry of Education and on the night of their departure to Bulgaria, they were put aboard the waiting plane. Shortly before take-off, Odinga appeared at the airport and as Vice President, ordered the Ministry of Education student contingent off the plane. He replaced them with fifty of his own selectees, and the plane left for Bulgaria. The Kenyan press had a field day with the incident, and later more serious charges surfaced when Odinga was suspected of plotting to overthrow of the government.

In 1966 he was forced to resign. He subsequently became leader of the Opposition in later years against the governments of Presidents Kenyatta and Moi.

Filemone Indire returned home from Moscow and after a further period with the Ministry of Foreign Affairs, he moved to the Ministry of Education and the Governing Council of the University of Nairobi to plan and establish the first School of Education in Kenya. Indire served as its first Dean until he was appointed by President Moi to one of the nominated seats in Parliament. A tall, portly man who exuded friendliness, Indire held several other posts over the years, such as Chairman of the University Senate and Chairman of the National Council for Science and Technology (NCST).

The other six recipients of the USA Government scholarships that year were Hannington Njeka Chite, John Mbugua (who travelled on the '59 Airlift), Harris Mule Mutio, Arthur Kwome Ojiambo, Appolonia Periera, I B Patel, and Peter Wambua.

Other women who went

Four women went privately, independent of the '59 Airlift. They were; Tabitha Gethaiga, Eva Ngaracu, Sarah Ngethe, and Margaret Karigaca. They were all bound for high school. Margaret was only fourteen years old in 1959. She had been scheduled to go on the Airlift, had raised the money, said her good-byes and then discovered at the airport that someone had removed her name from the list. Her father was so shaken that he rushed from the airport and did not return home until late that night. Margaret, bitterly disappointed, stayed in bed for the next two days and would not talk or eat.

On the following Monday, she and her father went to see Dr Kiano. When they told Kiano what had happened, he became so angry that he picked up a pencil from his desk and snapped it into two. He assured Margaret that she would go nonetheless and that he would give her the airfare himself. She arrived in California in time for the beginning of the second semester. When interviewed many years later, Margaret said, "So you can see why I owe everything to Dr Kiano."

Kiano arranged with the Scalapinos for Margaret to live in Berkeley with a woman friend of theirs and attend high school. At fourteen, she was the youngest to go to the United States. Understandably, she was terribly homesick the first few months, but the woman she lived with was like a mother to her. She comforted and encouraged her to stay.

She also took total responsibility for providing Margaret's support. Margaret finished junior and senior high school in Berkeley and went on to California State University East Bay at Hayward, California. All through college she worked – nights, weekends, and vacations – as a salesgirl at Sears. Again like so many others, she said this experience taught her the value of hard work and the undeniable importance of an education. It also made her realise that being a university student does not make one superior to others.

"Here in Kenya," she said, "they (university students) are waited on hand and foot, and come to expect it."

When Margaret finished her Bachelor's degree in Biology, she came straight home and joined the University of Nairobi for graduate work. She embarked on a career of teaching in Nairobi and eventually became the headmistress of State House Girls High School. By 1977, the senior staff of Kenya Girls High School, which had always been the premier girls' school in Kenya, was being Africanised. Margaret, a round-faced, energetic wife and mother of three, was appointed headmistress. When I interviewed her at the school in 1996, I was impressed by the high academic standards that were maintained and by the school's attractive physical appearance with its campus-like atmosphere. Imposing old stone buildings, surrounded by lawns and beautiful gardens, gave it an aura like that of leading private schools in the United States and Britain.

In addition to the four women who privately went that year and enrolled in high schools, three on the '59 Airlift attended high school as well. All of the women, including the total of thirteen who went on the Airlift and the four who went through other ways, obtained college degrees. All but two of the total of seventeen returned home. Beatrice Njuguna married a fellow Kenyan and settled in Washington State. The other lady Rose Gichoki, married a Nigerian. Many of the returnees were employed by the government in professional positions; Grace Wagema became Minister for Agriculture, Margaret Kabiru, and a number of others, became successful in business. Patricia Ododa was headmistress at Kisumu High School, and several other women taught in schools.

The most amazing story

Perhaps the most amazing saga of all was that of one student who managed, through an unlikely and near-miraculous series of events, to make his way privately to a college in California. Boaz Namasaka appeared at the Cultural Affairs Office door at USIS one morning in May

1959. He had travelled by bus for two days, from the then Bungoma District in Western Kenya to Nairobi, some 420 kilometres away and was dressed literally in rags. A strong smell of sweat accompanied him into my office. From inside his rags, Boaz pulled a third class Cambridge School Certificate, which would not have qualified him for admittance to any institution of higher learning in Kenya. He also had a letter of admission to Santa Barbara Junior College in California, which had a low tuition scholarship and accepted minimally qualified applicants. There was no promise of any financial help other than tuition, nor was Santa Barbara a residential college, meaning there would be no housing provided.

I attempted to explain this to Boaz, pointing out that he would need at least an additional USD$3,500 for his first year's expenses in order to accept the scholarship and be issued with a USA visa. Crestfallen, Boaz thanked me and left. I never expected to see him again.

In early August, Boaz appeared again, dressed as before. When I began painfully reiterating the requirements for a visa, Boaz pulled from his ragged clothing a most amazing array of currency: East African shillings, British pounds, traveller's cheques, and yes, American dollars. The fact that he had been able to raise so much money, and had travelled by bus with it hidden in his clothing, was truly astounding. When counted, the money amounted to more than the USD$3,500. Boaz explained that people in his village had held tea parties, local merchants were solicited, public appeals were made, and his family had sold precious land.

Stunned and impressed by this community effort, I immediately contacted Santa Barbara officials to make sure Boaz would get the kind of help he needed. Boaz raised additional funds to pay for his travel and left in September, 1959, for California. It soon became apparent to the people at Santa Barbara that he lacked the academic background for college level work, so they found him a family to live with and got him into a local high school. He graduated and went from there to Santa Barbara Junior College, then to Westmont College, where he graduated with a BA degree in History in 1967.

In 1969, Boaz obtained a master's degree from University of California, Los Angeles and in 1974 a PhD in History from Claremont College. He married Janet, a fellow Kenyan who had gotten her nursing degree in the USA. Boaz became a tenured professor at California State University at Fullerton. By 1982, he and Janet had well-paying jobs and four children, owned their own home and two cars, and were living the

American dream. But that year, Boaz suddenly announced that he wanted to go back to Kenya. Janet was reluctant to give up the life they had created, but Boaz insisted. "We now must go home," he told her.

With no jobs on the horizon, they came back to Kenya. Boaz was still negotiating for a university position in Kenya when he fell ill and died. Janet later discovered letters and laboratory results from the United States indicating that Boaz had Hodgkins Disease.[24] She could only assume that he had wanted to die in Kenya. A framed picture on the mantel of their modest Nairobi home showed a tall, regal-looking man in a handsome African robe.

> "He was an extraordinary man," Janet said. "He was very determined, always knew what he wanted and worked hard to get it. He didn't drink, saved his money, loved his children, and always helped with the cooking, housework, and childcare. He was a good man."

I will never forget Boaz, not only because of the professional success he achieved, but because of his indomitable spirit and his spectacular personal accomplishment against odds that had appeared insurmountable.

---

24 Hodgkin lymphoma is a cancer of the lymph tissue. The lymph tissue is found in the lymph nodes, spleen, liver, bone marrow, and other sites.

Chapter 8

Camelot and Kenya

Hyannisport, Massachusetts 26 July 1960

John Fitzgerald "Jack" Kennedy was unwinding after a strenuous six months of crisscrossing the country in his quest for the Democratic Party presidential nomination. Less than five days after winning it, he was about to receive a visitor from Africa, someone he had met at a conference in California in 1959. Perhaps he remembered the visitor as an interesting and articulate young man, and he may have been curious about the purpose of the visit, especially at that time.

That summer, newspapers were full of stories about crises in Africa. The Congo was exploding; revolts were breaking out in Angola; Rhodesia (now Zimbabwe) was coming apart at the seams; and in Kenya, African confrontation with white settlers was growing.

Kennedy's visitor that summer morning was Tom Mboya, who was in the United States to attend a General Assembly meeting of the United Nations. He was also on another mission. He hoped to enlist Kennedy's support for a second East African Student Airlift in 1960.

The appointment with Senator Kennedy had been hurriedly arranged by two of Mboya's American friends, Frank Montero and William Scheinman. Montero was a Democratic Party activist in New York and, as already mentioned in Chapter Five, he and Scheinman were board members of the American Committee on Africa (ACOA), whose mission was to "support African people in their struggle for freedom, independence, and economic justice." Montero initiated the meeting with Kennedy through his contacts with Pierre Salinger, Kennedy's press spokesman, and Kenny O'Donnell, another close aide.

That day in July, Scheinman chartered a plane and, along with Mboya, Montero, and Mboya's brother Alphonce Okuku, who was studying in the United States, flew to Hyannis early in the morning. They were met by a gaggle of Kennedy kids and in a caravan of cars proceeded to the Kennedy compound, past the ever-vigilant gaze of the press corps camped outside. The newsmen laying siege to the compound took only casual notice of what seemed to be neither a major international meeting nor one of much political interest.

According to Scheinman, Mboya and Kennedy did most of the talking. As Chairman of the Senate Foreign Relations Sub-Committee on African Affairs, Kennedy was genuinely interested in what was happening in Africa. In ensuing campaign speeches he would often make references to Africa's problems and the United States' concerns about them. Kennedy and Mboya chatted about Africa and its place in world politics for an hour or so before Kennedy brought the conversation around to the purpose of the visit.

Tom Mboya then laid out in detail the plight of a whole generation of Kenyan students who were being denied opportunities for higher education by the British colonial authorities, and who were being cast adrift into the Kenyan society just as the country was barrelling down the path towards independence. Without outside help it was inevitable that when independence did come to Kenya, Africans would lack the necessary training and education to run their country. A similar scenario had already been enacted elsewhere in Africa. The Congo (now Democratic Republic of Congo – DRC) had but twelve university graduates at the time of its independence from Belgium and suffered disastrous results as a consequence. These were perilous times for managing a new nation on the turbulent African continent. America, Mboya suggested, could help.

He told Senator Kennedy that the year before, in 1959, eighty-one students had left Kenya on the first, privately-funded 'East African Student Airlift', with scholarships to American universities and colleges. He then went on to explain that during that year, 1960, several hundred additional students had obtained admission and in some cases partial scholarships to colleges and universities in the United States and Canada. They were busy trying to raise money, in Kenya for their living expenses and books, but transport remained the major problem, and an exceedingly expensive one. Without travel money, the students would be unable to take up the college admissions and scholarships they had been awarded, and additionally, they could not obtain the necessary visas. Mboya's mission in the United States was to raise money for a second 'Airlift.'

He asked if the Senator could intercede with the State Department in Washington to help provide transport for the students. Previous appeals to Washington before the 1959 Airlift, and during the earlier months of 1960, had failed.

As the Democratic Party presidential candidate, the Senator had no illusions regarding this request.

"I'm the last guy in the United States to help you with the State Department today," he said.

He offered, however, to talk to Sargent Shriver, his brother-in-law and president of the Joseph P Kennedy, Jr Foundation, about the possibility of a grant from the Foundation, whose main purpose previously had been in the field of mental retardation. Shriver and Kennedy subsequently concluded that a grant was possible under the Foundation's charter, and Shriver contacted a number of major foundations, hoping to spark a cooperative effort.

The Kennedy Foundation grant

After getting a negative response from every foundation canvassed, Shriver and Kennedy reconsidered the grant question. Since it was now the beginning of August, time was of essence if students were to enrol by mid-September; so on 10 August 1960, Kennedy and Shriver committed USD$100,000 of the Joseph P Kennedy, Jr Foundation money to the airlift programme. The grant would be administered by the African-American Students Foundation (AASF), which Scheinman and Montero had established a year earlier with the express purpose of aiding East African students to study in the United States and Canada. A condition of the grant was that no public announcement be made; in order to keep it out of the political arena.

Nevertheless, news of the grant almost immediately became public, possibly leaked by a staffer at one of the foundations Shriver had contacted. By then, the presidential race was underway. When wind of the grant blew into the Republican tent, the political heat turned up markedly and led to some surprising results.

Senator Kennedy had been sincere in his attempt not to allow the Kennedy Foundation grant to the Airlift become a political football. He was genuinely interested in following the progress of the rising nationalist movements in Africa and elsewhere. But perhaps more than any other USA political leader of the time, he was aware of the tensions this created for the colonial powers of Europe and America's relations with its European friends.

The Republican Party, however, did not see the Kennedy initiative as anything but political gamesmanship, and so a furore erupted. On 13 August, a Time-Life staffer on loan to Richard Nixon for the political campaign – not about to be trumped by what he saw as a Democratic Party campaign ploy – began to lobby intensively for State Department funds to assist the project. Timing was becoming ever more critical, so after a flurry of high level contacts and conferences, the State Department on 15 August announced its willingness to commit USD$100,000 through the Institute of International Education (IIE) – the State Department's funding agent in those matters.

The rationale for the grant, as the State Department spokesman put it, was that, "Under these circumstances and in view of the current political situation in Africa, which makes it clearly of extreme importance, the United States should do everything in its power to emphasise its willingness to assist the people of Africa in every way ..."

It was the State Department's way of saving face, particularly since all prior requests for such assistance in 1959 and right up to 15 August 1960, had been rejected out of hand. Now, in this election year, the Department had reversed itself and amazingly found the money in only two days. Institutionally and bureaucratically, this quick response was unheard of, if not downright impossible. It was obvious that the decision was a political one. In previous years, in its regular scholarship programmes – Fulbright and Smith-Mundt – the State Department had not been willing to shift resources from Europe to provide additional scholarship assistance in Africa. This issue, with its political overtones, illustrates how quickly policy can be changed when an election year is in full swing.

The word about the State Department's as yet unannounced shift in policy went from the White House via Jackie Robinson, the former baseball star who was a strong Republican supporter and an AASF board member, to Frank Montero. Montero realised that grants from two sources, while tempting, might present AASF with something of a dilemma: a possible embarrassment of riches. Some members of the AASF board felt that both grants should be accepted; some argued for accepting only the private Kennedy Foundation grant; while others, particularly Jackie Robinson, who had played a key role in reversing the State Department's position, insisted that only the government grant be accepted. When consulted, however, Mboya expressed a strong desire that the project remains privately funded. He was influenced, no doubt, by the possibility of political fallout at home should he become closely associated with a United States Government-sponsored programme. He may also have feared the bureaucratic delays, red tape, and other restrictions that might have been placed on the programme. The AASF board accepted his recommendation.

After the board meeting, Montero called the State Department, which that same day had publicly announced the grant, and politely declined the offer. He indicated that the AASF preferred that the effort remains private.

With the election just two and a half months away, the issue of the grants hit the political fan and an immediate, firestorm ensued. On 17 August, Republican Senator Hugh Scott of Pennsylvania, from the floor of the United States Senate, attacked the Kennedy Foundation grant as an, "... apparent misuse of tax-exempt money for blatant political purposes." He added sarcastically, "But I can understand the pressures brought by the Kennedy people and their anxiety to take over the functions of the government in advance of the election."

Charge and counter charge flew across the Senate floor and were reported in detail by the media, especially *The New York Times* and *The Washington Post*. Senator Kennedy, in his defence on the Senate floor, stated, "I regard the statement made by the Senator from Pennsylvania as the most unfair, distorted, and malignant attack I have ever heard in fourteen years in politics."

Kennedy was followed by Senator J William Fulbright, Chairman of the Senate Foreign Relations Committee and the legislative author of the highly successful Fulbright Scholarship Programme (administered by the State Department). Senator Fulbright voiced his 'surprise' that a State Department grant of USD$100,000 could be made in just a few days, when he himself had been unsuccessful only recently in getting funds from the State Department to come to the aid of some Egyptian students. The State Department had, according to Senator Fulbright, claimed insufficient funds to honour his request despite his own urgings and those of the ambassador to Egypt.

Others weighed in with further explanations and charges, but by the end of August the political tempest subsided as the national campaign moved into high gear and the candidates, with the media in hot pursuit, turned to issues of greater concern to American voters.

Meanwhile, African students were up against the college admissions deadlines of mid-September. Thanks to the Kennedy Foundation grant, 288 Kenyans arrived in the Americas that September on the second East African Student Airlift. Later it became popularly known as the 'Kennedy Airlift.' Though the students were financed through the initiative of hundreds of private citizens in the United States and Canada, in addition to the pivotal Kennedy Foundation grant, the 1960 Airlift was most famous for its widely publicised Camelot-Kenya connection[25].

---

25 In American contexts, the word "Camelot" is sometimes used to refer admiringly to the presidency of John F Kennedy, as his term was said to have potential and promise for the future, and many were inspired by Kennedy's speeches, vision, and policies. At the time, Kennedy's assassination had been compared to the fall of King Arthur. The lines "Don't let it be forgot, that once there was a spot, for one brief shining moment, that was known as Camelot," from the musical Camelot, were quoted by his widow Jacqueline as being from his favourite song in the score. Source: Wikipedia

Chapter 9

The Kennedy Airlift, 1960

Organisation

The push for the 1960 Airlift was in response to the several hundred scholarships and offers of other assistance to Kenyan students that had emanated from the USA and Canada that year. All were the result of the combined efforts of Tom Mboya, Dr Kiano, Kariuki Njiiri, and the students themselves, the high visibility of the '59 Airlift, and the prodigious works of William Scheinman, Frank Montero, and others in the African American Students Foundation (AASF), whose efforts reached new heights following on the heels of their previous successful year.

The Kennedy Foundation placed their grant with the privately funded AASF and sent a team of Americans to oversee the project in Nairobi. The colonial officials refused to issue visas for Scheinman and Montero, fearing their reputation as activists, but allowed others to come including Albert Sims of the Institute of International Education (IIE), who headed the team. In the flurry of activity that followed, the bulk of the interviewing and last-minute fundraising was done by Tom Mboya, Dr Kiano, his wife Earnestine, Kariuki and Ruth Njiiri. No one worked harder than Mboya. According to one of the inspection team members, "Tom devoted himself indefatigably around the clock to the Airlift, organising and addressing innumerable fundraising events."

The team found that, thanks to the efforts of the African leaders, much of the support money for the students was raised in Kenya. About forty thousand dollars, came from the Asian community who were largely businessmen. The Aga Khan, head of the Ismailia sect of Islam and who had many followers in East Africa, donated fourteen thousand dollars.

Time was the enemy. As noted earlier, the Kennedy grant was not made until mid-August, less than four weeks before the students were due to report to their institutions. One of the biggest problems was lack of information. Just like in 1959, it had to be determined which students had been admitted to which schools, proof of admission, how much money they had and how much more they would need, who had passports and who met the criteria for visa approval. And just how many students were there, anyway? How many planes would they need – three? Four? All this had to come together before anyone boarded the aircrafts bound for New York on 15 September.

In the midst of this chaos, the Kennedy Foundation team, the colonial Department of Education, the American Consular officials, and the African leadership including many volunteers like Ruth Njiiri and Earnestine Kiano, mounted a round-the-clock effort to bring this Airlift to fruition. It was determined at the last minute that a fourth aircraft was needed to take the final total of 288 students to New York.

Where the students went

Those who went on this Airlift were not much different from the ones who had gone the year before, except that there were so many more of them, a few of whom were from other parts of Eastern and Southern Africa. Over three hundred fifty students arrived in the US that year, seventy of whom went privately. The rest went on the Airlift, filling four planes. Thirty three were from Tanganyika, nine from Uganda, and one each from Northern Rhodesia (Zambia) and Nyasaland (Malawi). The rest were from Kenya. A total of fifty three women went that year, a majority of whom, again, were on their way to high schools.

The '60 Airlift students spread across the United States and Canada, going to almost every state, including Alaska. Many attended schools where Kenyans had gone before: the Wisconsin State Colleges, Lincoln University in Pennsylvania, Philander-Smith, Indiana University, Tuskegee, Greenville College, Earlham College, and Diablo Community College. Others attended Cornell University, Brandeis, Bowling-Green, Bryn Mawr, Colby, the University of Michigan, and Skidmore College. A good number went to church-related schools such as the Wesleyan colleges across the US, Catholic colleges and academies, and Baptist, Lutheran, and Quaker schools. Many of the members in the 1960 group were bound for high schools than ever before.

Contrary to dire predictions in Britain, in Kenya, and even in the USA, the vast majority of students returned home after completing their education. Only eight (approximately 3.4%) were known to have stayed in the United States.

Again, like the '59 returnees, many of the graduates went into government positions being vacated by British colonial civil servants, while others were co-opted in business and industry, journalism, teaching, higher education, the church, politics, agriculture, and new social institutions and cultural organisations. A number became Members of Parliament and occupied ministerial positions in Commerce and Industry, Finance, Health, Local Government, and Natural Resources. One of the Kennedy Airlift students, Perez Olindo, became a long time director of the Kenya Wildlife Conservation and Management Department. Given that the tourism industry was Kenya's number one source of foreign exchange revenue (followed by agriculture) because of the magnificent variety of big game, his job was a crucial one.

Another '60 Airlift graduate, Zacchaeus Chesoni, became a High Court judge and was later Chief Justice of Kenya and chairman of the Electoral Commission of Kenya. He died on 5 September 1999.

Philip Wangalwa became the Deputy Editor of the *Daily Nation*, the country's leading newspaper. Aron Kandie was Director of Personnel in the office of the President, while others became general managers, executive directors, high civil servants, and permanent secretaries in various ministries. Kenya's Foreign Service also drew on the 1960 Airlift. For instance, Sospeter Mageto started his education at Alcorn A & M College in Mississippi, and later went back as Kenya's ambassador to the United States. Several others eventually achieved the same rank. The staffing of all levels of government and business by the students who made up the Airlifts of 1959, 1960, and 1961, as well as the other American graduates, was critical to the implementation of major changes in the operations of an African society and a new nation.

Success stories

Some of the greatest success stories came from the women on the '60 Airlift, including Priscilla Njeri and Josephine Kamau, who were discussed in earlier chapters. They all played a key role in bringing revolutionary changes to the social order in Kenya by reshaping family life and having careers of their own, particularly in business and education.

One of those ladies was Lucy Kago, who experienced some of the negative as well as the positive aspects of living and studying in the USA. Her father was a well respected teacher and educational administrator and in 1959 was the first African to be sent by USIS to participate in a three month teacher training programme in the United States. Lucy had graduated from Alliance Girls High school and from a teacher training college in Kenya, where she had trained as a primary teacher. Her first school in the USA was Wayland Baptist College in Texas. A sturdy, scholarly looking woman in glasses, she described her experience there in graphic terms. She was shunned on campus, treated like a servant, and expected to follow the Texas Jim Crow[26] laws of the time. Vocal, proud, and an early feminist, Lucy was not the type of woman to endure such treatment.

"They were Baptists but they weren't very Christian," she said, shaking her head and setting her cluster of cornrows flying. "They treated me badly. I was already a qualified teacher and I said I would not put up with such treatment. I said I would not stay there but would go home."

Instead, the African American Institute (AAI) in New York moved her after one semester to the University of New Hampshire.

"It was like going from one extreme to the other," she said. "The people in New Hampshire treated me very well. A family there befriended me and were like my adopted parents. They live in Maine now (2013) and I visit them whenever I go to the United States."

In September 1960, right after the Airlifters landed in New York City, Lucy was chosen to present a hand carved Kisii stool to President Kennedy as a token of their gratitude for his assistance to the Airlift. She was invited some time later to the Kennedy compound in Hyannisport to meet some of the Kennedy family. She remembered it as the most lasting impression of her time in the USA.

Lucy earned a BA degree in Biology from the University of New Hampshire in 1964, followed by a three month teacher certification course at Columbia University. On returning to Kenya, she taught Science at Alliance Girls High School and later headed the National Science Curriculum project at the Kenya Institute of Education (KIE) – now Kenya Institute of Curriculum Development (KICD). In 1988 she became Director of Education at the National Museums of Kenya (now Nairobi National Museum). She married John Ndegwa, a librarian at the University of Nairobi. In addition to her successful career, she is a mother of three children.

Another woman who became an outstanding leader of change was Helen Wamere Mwangi. She was born in Dr Kiano's home area of Murang'a, where her father was a teacher. She finished first in her class at Alliance Girls High School and was one of the rare women selected for acceptance at Makerere College. After two years there, she decided she wanted to go to America. An American friend of Ruth and Kariuki

26 The laws mandated *de jure* segregation in all public facilities, with a supposedly "separate but equal" status for black Americans.

Njiiri, Amelia Thomas, happened to be visiting them in Kenya at the time. A Bryn Mawr College alumna, she was so impressed when she met Wamere that she immediately lobbied Bryn Mawr for a scholarship for her. Wamere's outstanding record won her a full scholarship, but she still needed travel money as well as the several hundred dollars for her first year's expenses required by the USA Consulate.

Her father was no longer a teacher, having been brutally beaten and left for dead by Mau Mau insurgents during the Emergency period. Missionaries saved his life, but he felt unable to return to teaching. Instead, he became an evangelist and travelled around Kenya preaching. When he was called home from Kisumu to deal with Wamere's money problems, he gathered the family around him to pray, and then announced to his daughter, "I have no money to give you, but we have prayed to the Lord and he knows your problem. It is now in his hands."

With that, he went back to Kisumu to preach.

Wamere cried for three days, until a letter came from Bryn Mawr College promising her seven hundred dollars for expenses. "So," she said with a laugh during a 1988 interview, "perhaps the prayers worked after all!"

With the help of the Njiiris, Dr Kiano, and Tom Mboya, a place on the Kennedy Airlift was promised, and Wamere attended Bryn Mawr. She graduated in 1963 with a degree in Philosophy and French. She wanted to stay at Bryn Mawr to work on a doctorate, but no scholarship was available. Instead, with help again from Mboya, she was offered a scholarship by the French Embassy to Aix-en-Provence. Interestingly, she was the only Kenyan African at that time who could speak French.

"That was a bad day for me," she said. "I was so unhappy. I did not want to leave Bryn Mawr." Neither did she want to leave Amelia Thomas, who had become "like a mother to me."

But after three years in Aix-en-Provence she had completed her doctorate in Philosophy and French except for her thesis. At this point she married a Congolese named Dadet and went with him to Brazzaville. Her husband entered the Congo's Foreign Service and Wamere stayed in Brazzaville to become Chairperson of the Department of Modern Languages. The marriage ended in divorce in 1978 and Wamere and her three children returned to Kenya where she became a lecturer at Kenyatta University. By 1987 she was Chairperson of the Department of Foreign Languages. She was also Chairperson of the Board of Governors of a boys' high school and on the Board of three other high schools.

I interviewed Wamere, a slender, attractive woman, on the shady veranda of her University staff flat, where she reflected on her years in the USA. She had worked during the summers as a clerk at Beth Israel Hospital in Boston and at a local trade union office of the AFL/CIO in Philadelphia. Both were rewarding experiences, teaching her to be independent and not expect to lean on the network of aunties, uncles, and extended family the way many Kikuyu people did. At the same time, she also learnt the value of working cooperatively in groups for the benefit of all.

"I think we all learnt from our American experience that we can accomplish much more if we work together to solve the problems of our society and the environment," she said.

Another notable student on the 1960 Airlift was Wangari Maathai, winner of the 2004 Nobel Peace Prize for 'her contribution to sustainable development, democracy and peace' through environmental work in Kenya. She had a long and impressive career in Kenya. She received a scholarship at Mount St Scholastica College (now Benedictine College) in Atchison, Kansas, and after graduation went on to the University of Pittsburgh for a Master's degree in Biology. She returned to Kenya in 1969, where she became the first woman in East and Central Africa to earn a PhD and the first woman to chair a university department (the Department of Veterinary Anatomy at the University of Nairobi.) She established the Green Belt Movement that resulted in the planting of millions of trees all over Kenya to prevent soil erosion and preserve the environment, and that led to her winning the Nobel Peace Prize. A determined activist for the civil rights of Africans and an outspoken critic of the government of President Daniel arap Moi, she was imprisoned more than once for her defence of democracy and especially of the rights of women. She was elected to Parliament in the free elections of 2002, and in 2003 was appointed Assistant Minister for the Environment prior to receiving the Nobel Prize in 2004. She died in 2011.

Others who went privately

Besides the men and women who went to the USA on the Kennedy Airlift, sixty-nine others obtained various kinds of sponsorships as interest in Africa grew and scholarships in the United States became more. In 1960, the Inter-American University at San German, Puerto Rico, offered Kenyans not one but seven full scholarships including travel. The recipients included James Mburu Kangongoi, Johnny Wallace

Karungu, Damian Cosmos Kungu, Lawrence Mwathi, Crispus Ndeli, James Njuhigu, and Zachary Onyonka. Onyonka, who came from Kisii, described his experience at Inter-American University as extremely happy, in a climate much like Kenya's where he made many friends among both faculty and students. He particularly liked the open, cross-cultural, cosmopolitan atmosphere of the university. He completed his BA degree in 1963, and went on to an internship at the United Nations in New York for a few months before entering graduate school to study Economics. Originally scheduled to go to Northeastern University, he changed his mind when he learnt that Syracuse University had a programme of East African Studies and a good Economics department. By 1965, he had his MA degree and a Rockefeller Scholarship to work on a PhD. With only his dissertation to do, he was offered a lectureship position at the University of Nairobi, where he spent a year before returning to Syracuse to complete his doctorate.

Shortly thereafter, Onyonka was elected to Parliament and was launched on an outstanding ministerial career. He was first Minister for Economic Planning, later Minister for Information and Broadcasting, then Minister for Health, Minister for Education then Minister for Housing and Social Services. Re-elected to Parliament in 1983, he became Minister for Foreign Affairs in 1987, and following that Minister for Research, Science and Technology. When I interviewed him in 1988, he took great satisfaction in noting that five of the Permanent Secretaries in Kenya's ministries at that time were his students in Economics during that brief time in 1967-68 when he was a lecturer at the University of Nairobi. In 1988, he had the longest continuous record of service as a Member of Parliament in the government with the exception of President Moi and President Kibaki.

Onyonka's distinguished career was recognised by his alma mater in 1981 when he was awarded an honorary degree by Syracuse University, sharing the platform with another recipient, General Alexander Haig, former US Secretary of State. Such a record of achievement is especially remarkable in view of the fact that he began his career, without apprenticeship, immediately after completing his graduate studies.

Importance of the Airlifts

Certainly by the time these graduates from the 1959, 1960, and later 1961 Airlifts returned home, Kenya was undergoing a major sea change. From the first election of Africans to the Legislative Council in 1957 until independence in 1963, the political and economic turmoil was immense. The shift from settler and Colonial Office control to the acceptance and incorporation of Africans into all facets of public and economic life became the dynamic. The role of educated Africans, including the women, became increasingly important with the formation of a coalition government and internal self-rule in 1962, and was even more crucial after independence. Although they were, like Zachary Onyonka, thrust without the benefit of much apprenticeship into significant positions of leadership in the fledgling nation, this generation of educated Africans was not awed by the tasks before them. Through their experiences abroad, they had gained the assurance that they could tackle any problem and succeed.

Chapter 10

The last Airlift, 1961

Organising the last Airlift

The third and last Airlift took off from Nairobi in 1961, but, unlike the two previous Airlifts, it received official American government sanction through the US State Department's agent, the Institute of International Education (IIE). This Airlift was organised by professional educators. Politicians in Kenya were not involved in the selection of students, though they continued to raise funds and solicit scholarships. Under IIE's leadership, several educational agencies came together to form a consortium – the Council for Educational Cooperation with Africa (CECA). Members included IIE, the African-American Institute (AAI), the African Scholarship Programme of American Universities (ASPAU), the African-American Students Foundation (AASF), and the Phelps-Stokes Fund. Assistant Secretary of State for Educational and Cultural Affairs Philip Coombs approved CECA's proposal to provide support for students from East and Central Africa, and the USA government pledged USD$100,000 for the programme. The colonial government in Kenya, assured of the non-political nature of the Airlift, gave UK£5,000 pounds sterling. Gordon Hagberg, who was with AAI in Washington at the time, was recruited to coordinate the Airlift as head of the CECA team. By this time, I was back in Washington at the State Department's Bureau of Educational and Cultural Affairs and keeping track of the Airlift activity from there.

Tom Mboya once again travelled to the United States to raise money and find scholarships for the ever increasing numbers of students seeking higher education in America. This time, with Kennedy as President and an administration sympathetic to African aspirations, Mboya was willing to accept USA government involvement in a programme he was formerly determined to keep under private control.

CECA's counterpart in Kenya, which would constitute the liaison with Hagberg's team, was the Kenya Education Fund (KEF). Participants in the KEF included the Kenya Education Trust, the Kenya Women's

Scholarship Fund, and the Nairobi office of the African-American Students Foundation. Board members of KEF were Mboya, Munyua Waiyaki, Kariuki and Ruth Njiiri, Dr Mungai Njoroge, and Dr J Likimani.

As a leading African Member of Parliament, Mboya was that year involved in high level government meetings where the first steps towards independence were being discussed. He nevertheless continued his efforts at fundraising. He even sold pictures of Jomo Kenyatta at a Kenyan Education Fund rally in Nairobi City Stadium, where the future president made one of his first appearances after his release from detention. Local merchants and businesses in Kenya contributed funds, and the students themselves raised as much as fifty thousand US dollars from friends, relatives, and their home villages. As Gordon Hagberg wrote in his report to CECA, "This is in the best 'help those who help themselves' tradition cherished by Americans."

Students on the Airlift

In the end, enough money was raised from all sources to send four planeloads of students to the United States and Canada in September. Again, there were over three hundred, about 16% of whom were women. Once again, they came from all over Kenya, but also some from the other countries in Eastern and Central Africa. The governments of Tanganyika and Uganda contributed their share of the airfares for students from their two countries.

Gordon Hagberg, in his report, gave a summary of the students' varied backgrounds. Most, he said, were primary school teachers and clerks, but there were also secretaries, draughtsmen, laboratory assistants, surveyors, postal clerks, salesmen, and health inspectors. In his book, _Freedom and After_, Tom Mboya quotes Hagberg's description of their departure:

"... there were thousands on hand at the airport. Spontaneous singing and dancing, and the excited chatter of old and young, made a happy bedlam of the otherwise austere airport building."

An outstanding 1961 Airlifter

The students dispersed to the usual broad spectrum of high schools and colleges in the United States and Canada, from Seward High School in Alaska to Harvard University in Massachusetts. Many achieved outstanding success. An example is Stephen Kimani, whose accomplishments in the field of medicine were impressive. He first went to Worcester Polytechnic Institute in Massachusetts where he received a Bachelor of Science degree in Chemistry. He then moved on to George Washington University in Washington DC for a Master of Science degree in Physiology, then to Thomas Jefferson University in Philadelphia, Pennsylvania for a PhD in Human Physiology, and finally to Michigan State University for his MD. He spent five years in a residency programme in General Surgery at Harlem Hospital Centre of the Columbia University College of Physicians and Surgeons, where he was responsible for the diagnosis and management of all trauma and elective general surgery cases. After his return to Kenya, he became a lecturer in the Department of Medical Physiology at the University of Nairobi, opened his own clinic on the outskirts of Nairobi, and was appointed Executive Director of the Tropical Health Institute, a non-governmental organisation whose objective was to provide health programmes for rural communities.

One final story

One final story of luck, stubborn perseverance, and eventual triumph over the odds seems an appropriate way to end this chronicle of many such tales during an extraordinary era. Samuel Macharia, despite all his best efforts, did not get a seat on the 1961 Airlift. Though he was accepted with a scholarship at Seattle Technical College, when he applied for an Airlift seat he was told that he would need East African shillings 4,000/- (about USD$570 at the time) for expenses. His father sold land and Samuel's village held *harambees* (parties or rallies where everyone chips in some money), but he still lacked East African shillings 2,000/-, and the plane left without him.

Samuel was however, not unaccustomed to overcoming obstacles. During his childhood he had survived even greater misfortune. His father, a Kikuyu, had taken the family to live in Arusha, Tanganyika, where he had found work on a farm. Unfortunately, this was during the outbreak of the Mau Mau rebellion, and one day some British colonial officers from Kenya appeared and rounded up all the Kikuyu people in the area. They put them and their families in lorries and shipped them back to Kenya.

To Samuel's family's great distress, six-year-old Samuel was out tending cattle with some of his Maasai friends, and he was left behind. The local Maasai tribesmen looked after him and helped him along the way as he travelled from *manyatta* to *manyatta* (Maasai compounds) on a long, three-year journey North to find his family. Amazingly enough he succeeded. During our interview Samuel said that, even so many years later, his father still cried when he told this story.

Samuel had attended primary school through Standard eight and then went to a teacher training school, during which time he corresponded with a number of schools in the United States. Though he lacked formal secondary education, he was nevertheless given the scholarship to Seattle Technical College.

When he failed to get aboard the Airlift, he sought other ways to get to the USA. Eventually he found an Indian travel agent in Nairobi who was arranging travel for Indians fleeing to England in advance of Kenya's independence, as they feared they would be expelled to India when the British left. The travel agent agreed to help him. Samuel withdrew his two thousand East Africa shillings from his father's postal account (without telling his father) and gave them to the agent, who provided him with application forms for a passport and an American visa. He also gave Samuel an air ticket to help convince the authorities that he had the wherewithal to go. The passport and visa were issued, though how he managed to bypass the requirement of several hundred US dollars for his first year's expenses remains a mystery. When he returned to the Indian agent, the man tore up the air ticket and told Samuel to be at his office at five o'clock the following day where transport would be provided.

At the appointed hour, Samuel found four large buses in front of the agent's office, along with many Indians. They all boarded the buses and headed West towards Uganda, then North to the Southern Sudan. Samuel did not remember how long it took, but he said they spent many days and nights on the buses. Somewhere in Sudan they were floated across the Nile on logs loosely tied together, wondering if their bare legs would invite attacks from the crocodile-infested waters.

On the other side of the river, more buses waited. Samuel and the Indians were taken to Khartoum, then on through Egypt to Libya. All Samuel could remember eating during the whole long trip across Africa was bread and bananas. In Libya, the bus passengers were put aboard a boat and taken across the Mediterranean to a 'small country'. Samuel did not know its name – possibly Monaco. They boarded buses once again and were driven across Europe to France, thence on the ferry to Dover, and then to London.

This was the end of the journey for all but Samuel, who was the only one going on to the United States. Samuel did not know how, but somehow the Indian agent had arranged for him to get a ticket to New York. He landed there in June, 1962, 142 days after leaving Nairobi.

He had no money and no idea where Seattle was; much less that it was almost five thousand kilometres away. A stranger pointed him towards the Greyhound Bus Station, where he explained his dilemma to two New York policemen. They took him to the police station, where he was allowed to stay for several days until some stranger – he did not know who – bought him a bus ticket to Seattle.

On his arrival there, after nine days on the bus, he learnt that the couple with whom the school had arranged for him to stay had gotten a divorce and both had moved. Samuel lived for a short time with another Kenyan student's host family, but the place proved too crowded, and he had to move out. He was finally able to contact the woman, who was to be his original host, and she put him up temporarily in an empty building with no facilities – no food, water, or heat.

A local Presbyterian church heard of his plight and came to his rescue. A new host family was found, and Samuel stayed with them for nine years. He worked the whole time, mostly in a factory making glass bottles, while at the same time going to school. He made up the high school credits he lacked, received his diploma, and in 1969 earned a BA degree from Seattle University. He also achieved another goal that same year when he became a Certified Public Accountant, followed by a master's degree from the University of Washington in 1972.

In 1973, Samuel was recruited by one of the Kenya manpower teams touring the United States, and he returned to Kenya. He worked as an accountant and financial officer in various government offices and private businesses, including a stint in the Agricultural Development Corporation. On a trip to Italy in the 1970s to study how to improve Kenya's beef stock, he was struck by some Italian farmers' simple technology for manufacturing inexpensive toilet paper. He realised that the majority of rural Kenyans did not use the costly toilet paper imported from England, and upon his return home, he borrowed enough money from the National Bank of Kenya to start his own toilet paper mill. It was a phenomenal success, with eventually three more paper mills going full blast.

His career took an abrupt turn however, when in 1992 he became interested in politics and saw the power of radio to influence the election campaigns that year. It took him several years to get a radio license. He ultimately had to agree to support President Daniel arap Moi in exchange for being granted the license by the government.

In 1998 his first radio station went on the air. The following years saw many ups and downs. Despite his alleged support for Moi, Samuel's station was shut down more than once for its outspoken criticism of corruption in the President's government. In 2002 he switched his support to Mwai Kibaki, who was elected president that year to replace President Moi.

"I just turned like a chameleon at the end of 2002," he was quoted saying.

Samuel subsequently became a highly successful media mogul. He not only still controls the biggest broadcast network in Kenya – Citizen Radio, several other radio stations and TV stations through his Royal Media Services Company, but also once owned a newspaper.

From a small boy herding cattle with his Maasai friends, and a bare-legged youth crossing the Nile on a raft, he had made the amazing leap to the peak of the media industry in Kenya.

Chapter 11

Summing up the Airlifts

There can be no doubt that both the immediate and the long-range impact of the three Airlifts were enormous. The United States reaped the cross-cultural benefits of having these young African students living, working, and studying among them, and Americans learnt more about a little-known but important part of the world. In doing so, they were able as a nation to foster friendly relations with many of the leaders of Kenya. These relations persist to this day. Derek Bok, president of Harvard University, emphasised this when he said in 1976,

"Our universities have become the most attractive places in the world in which to get advanced training. As a result, we have the opportunity to train much of the future leadership of the underdeveloped world. To capitalise on this opportunity could be extremely valuable, not because students who study here will necessarily love America and agree with our policies when they return to their native countries, but simply because it will be easier to conduct government and commercial relationships with persons who are better trained and who understand our language and our culture."

In Kenya, the Airlifts had an impact not only on the students who made the almost unimaginable transition from their rural villages to the highest realms of government, business, and academia, but also on the development of the country itself. Had not these hundreds of American and Canadian graduates been available when independence came, one wonders what would have happened to Kenya.

One possibility would have been government ministries with Africans as figureheads at the helm, but the real power and authority remaining in the hands of colonial civil servants, who would then stay on for many years.

Another possibility would have been the rise to power of a ruthless dictator like Idi Amin in Uganda or Mobutu Sese Seko in the Congo. Whatever the course of events, it would have been significantly different had there been a vacuum created by the absence of the American-educated leaders.

The generations of Kenyans who followed would have been seriously affected too. Today, the literacy rate in Kenya is 84-87%, but under a pseudo-independent government still run by British colonial officers and white settlers, little might have been done to provide any more education for Africans than had been done in the past. The Africanisation process in all areas of government and society could not have happened without trained personnel, and the discontent of the Africans might have erupted in civil chaos (which has happened recently for different reasons) or even in a Mau Mau-like uprising.

Instead, with the wise counsel of President Kenyatta, who urged Kenyans both black and white to put the past behind them and go forward together, the new, independent Kenya, led by American-trained graduates in every sector, enjoyed more than a decade of prosperity and stability. Though there were no more Airlifts, educational opportunities abroad greatly expanded from 1962 onwards, and hundreds of Kenyan students continued to go overseas to study. By the late 1960s the number had skyrocketed to about five thousand, and in the 2001/2002 academic year, it had grown to more than seven thousand. Many of the first waves of students have sent their children to college in the States, and over the years a reservoir of pro-American sentiments has been created in a generally hostile world. It is an asset the United States would do well to foster and preserve.

Of the three African political leaders who helped conceive, organise, and bring the Airlifts to fruition, Dr Julius Gikonyo Kiano was the only one who lived long enough to serve the government of independent Kenya for many years and in many capacities, including, as noted, a number of cabinet ministries. He died of a heart attack in 2003. The untimely death of Tom Mboya came in 1969, cutting short his role as an influential leader in Kenyan politics. Kariuki Njiiri, in 1962, gave up his seat in Parliament in favour of Jomo Kenyatta, who became Prime Minister in June that year and the first president of the Republic of Kenya in December, 1964. Njiiri was rewarded with a post as party publicity secretary for the Kenya African National Union (KANU). He died in a car accident in 1975.

It is because of the dedication of these three to the cause of higher education for Kenyans that so many of their fellow countrymen and women have been able to contribute so much for so long to the well-being of Kenya. Their legacy lives on in the immensely expanded opportunities for the present and future generations of Kenyans.

Bibliography

The Private Papers and Interview Notes of Robert F. Stephens.

The Speeches of Senator John F. Kennedy, Presidential Campaign of 1960.

Bok, Derek C. Address to the Harvard Alumni of Mexico City. 1976.

Matheson, Alistair. "The Kenyan – US Student Airlift." Unpublished occasional paper, Nairobi, 1986.

Elkins, Caroline. *Britain's Gulag: The Brutal End of Empire in Kenya*. London: Jonathan Cape, 2005.

Gatheru, R. Mugo. *Child of Two Worlds*. London: Heinemann, 1966.

Goldsworthy, David. *Tom Mboya: The Man Kenya Wanted to Forget*. London: Heinemann, 1982.

Kenyatta, Jomo. *Facing Mount Kenya: The Tribal Life of the Gikuyu*. New York: Vintage, 1965.

Maathai, Wangari Muta. *Unbowed: A Memoir*. New York: Knopf, 2006.

Mboya, Tom. *The Challenge of Nationhood: A Collection of Speeches and Writings*. London: Heinemann, 1970.

Mboya, Tom. *Freedom and After*. London: Andre Deutsch Limited, 1963.

Obama, Barack. *Dreams from My Father: A Story of Race and Inheritance*. New York: Three Rivers Press, 2004.

Ogot, Bethwell. *Historical Dictionary of Kenya*. Metuchan, New Jersey and London: The Scarecrow Press, Inc., 1981.

Rampersad, Arnold. *Jackie Robinson: A Biography*. New York: Knopf, 1997.

Smith, Mansfield. "The East African Airlifts of 1959, 1960 and 1961." Thesis, Syracuse University, 1966.

Webbink, Jane B. *African Students at Soviet Universities*. Policy Research Study, U.S. Department of State, 1964.

Were G.S. and Wilson, D.A. *East Africa Through a Thousand Years*. London: Evans Brothers, Limited, 1968.

Index